MW01614440

CHANGING LENSES
Essential Teaching Stories
from Ram Dass

Introduction

I first heard Ram Dass speak in Montreal in the winter of 1969. He had just returned from India the year before and began his lecture circuit around the US and Canada. Eight months later, I followed him back to India to meet our guru, Neem Karoli Baba. That trip completely changed the course of my life and years later I started to work with Ram Dass on preserving and spreading his vast collection of teachings.

Ram Dass has lived a captivating life ripe with experience and deep transmissions from some of the most awake beings of this century. He has woven his life experiences with these timeless teachings to create a tapestry of stories filled with humor, poignancy and profound insight that provide a common ground for so many people to clearly see their own imperfect human tendencies.

In this anthology we have gathered together Ram Dass' 'classics' and 'rarities', enabling the reader to absorb the deepest essence of meaning that these stories can provide.

May these tales help you to unravel the great mystery and provide you a path to revelation and joy.

Namaste
Raghu Markus

©2018 Love Serve Remember Foundation
2355 Westwood Blvd #130 Los Angeles Ca 90064
ISBN 978-0-9992338-2-5

Compiled and Edited by Noah Markus
Designed by Zoë Kors
Produced by Raghu Markus and Rachael Fisher
Special thanks to Marlene Roeder and Joanne Baughan for curating these stories.

Collage artwork by Marissa de Leon
www.artbymdl.com
@art_by_mdl
Inspired by Perception of David

The following photos that appear within the artistic collages of this book can be attributed to the following:

Page 8 - © Rameshwar Das Lytton
Page 11 - © Love Serve Remember Foundation
Page 43 - © Love Serve Remember Foundation
Page 49 - © Love Serve Remember Foundation
Page 62 - © Rameshwar Das Lytton
Page 74 - © Kathleen Murphy
Page 81 - © Rameshwar Das Lytton
Page 91 - © Love Serve Remember Foundation
Page 97 - © Peter Simon (PeterSimon.com)
Page 112 - © Balaram Das Goetsch

RamDass.org
Contact: info@RamDass.org

All Rights Reserved. No part of this book may be reproduced in any form
or by any electronic or mechanical means. Including information storage and
retrieval systems, without permission in writing by the author.

Side A:
The Classics

Side A: The Classics

Yogi Biscuits

My guru used to show me that he knew what was in my mind. I don't know how to describe it. Maybe a story will give you a feeling for it.

In 1968, after I had been at the Temple in the mountains for about three or four months, I was allowed to go to Delhi to extend my visa. I was a yogi by then; I mean, I was really into being a yogi. I was incredibly high from doing long fasts and many hours of meditation. I was wearing a potato-sack type thing, and I had beads and a long beard, long hair. I was barefoot, and I was walking through Delhi. It's quite a phenomenon. Sadhus or those kinds of holy people are very respected in India. And when you're a Western one, it's a double whammy because they figure you're a king, you've got all this money, so what are you doing here? They really respect you. I went into a stationery store to get some envelopes, and I went into my jola – my bag – to get the money, and the man said, "Oh, no, no, no. We wouldn't take money from you!"

I said, "Why not? I'm a Westerner. I have money."

"Oh, no, no, I can feel your spirit. I wouldn't take money from you. It's an honor to serve you." So I'm walking barefoot through the streets, I'm just floating out there, and I suddenly realize I'm in a different universe than I had been when I'd been in Delhi before.

It came time for lunch, and I decided to go to a vegetarian restaurant, a good restaurant, as yogis should. I went in, and again they were very respectful. They sat me down in a booth, and they were all kind of watching me. I got caught in my ego, along with the bliss I was feeling, and I began to be aware of them watching me be a holy man. So when I offered the food, I offered it with a little bit of show biz, just kind of put a little schmaltz into it. They served me an appropriate yogi meal, and I ate yogi-like. Everybody was very pleased, because I was very holy.

Then the dessert came, and it was sherbet. And in it were these two cream-filled English biscuits. I hadn't had those in a long time, and I really wanted them. Now I knew they weren't yogi food – and I knew they knew it, too. But I wanted those biscuits so bad! There was a fat little Jewish boy from Boston who wanted those biscuits. I mean, the yogi didn't want them, you can't badmouth him. He was just sitting there being holy. But this little Jewish boy, he wanted them!

But they were watching . . .

So I looked holy in this direction, and I edged the dessert around to the left, and then I turned as if I were doing something holy in that direction, and I sort of slipped the cookies into my mouth so they wouldn't see it. I got the two cookies eaten, and managed to get my holiness out of the restaurant, and that night I took the all-night bus back up to Nainital.

The next day I took the bus out to see my guru. I brought apples, and I offered him the apples. He was talking to somebody, then he turned and looked at me and said, "How did you like the biscuits?"

Nodding in Agreement

I've told the story many times, but it's such a delicious story. In the '70s when I was lecturing, everybody wore white and smiled a lot and had flowers in their hair, and they were all between 15 and 25 years old; that's what the Explorers Club looked like in those days. One evening there was a woman sitting down in the front, and she was probably around 70. She was wearing a little hat with flowers and plastic strawberries and cherries on it, a print dress, and responsible-looking Oxfords, a black patent leather bag, and a net on her hair. She was very different than the rest of the audience. As I looked around the room, I thought, There's somebody's grandmother. Obviously someone said, "Hey, Grandma, you ought to come hear this guy," and she did it. She's a hip grandma.

I started to report to the Explorers Club what had been going on in my inner journey. In those days we all "knew." We were the people who "knew," and it was just a matter of time until . . . do you remember those days? Tim Leary and I had a chart on the wall of how soon everybody would get enlightened.

I started to tell the kind of far-out stories that all of us who knew, knew, and as I looked around once I saw her nodding along. I thought, How does she know? She doesn't look like an acid head! So I'd tell sort of a more extreme story: "I was on acid, in Mexico, in the ocean, in the middle of the night, and I had this experience where the thread of life was cut . . ."

I look, and she's nodding away. So I figure, Well, maybe she's got a neck problem. Maybe that's why she's nodding. I watched to see if she nodded after a story or nodded at other times; I got fascinated with her! By the end of the lecture, I couldn't resist. I smiled at her and kind of beckoned her to come up. She came up to the front and said, "Oh, thank you so much! That's just the way I understand things to be."

I said, "How do you know? What have you done in your life that has been your practice that allows you to know these things?"

She leaned forward very conspiratorially and said, "I crochet."

At that moment I knew that the game was a different one than I thought it was. So you appreciate that while my route through happened to be chemicals, obviously crocheting gets you to just the same place.

Take It to Delhi

My car broke down and Maharajji said, "Take it to Delhi to have it fixed."

I thought, What does he know about cars? I'll have it fixed here in Nainital. So they tried and they tried and they couldn't fix it. I went to Maharajji and said, "They can't fix the car in Nainital."

Maharajji said, "Take it to Delhi."

I said, "Maharajji, it would mean renting a truck to put it on and driving 200 miles to Delhi!"

Maharajji said, "Take it to Delhi."

Again I thought, What does he know about cars? He's a silly old man. There was a Volkswagen repair place in Almora. So I contacted them, and for weeks they wouldn't come. I went back to Maharajji and said, "The Volkswagen people in Almora won't come. They're German mechanics."

Maharajji said, "Take it to Delhi."

So I finally figured, all right, I'll take it to Delhi. We rented a truck and put the car aboard; Krishna Das drove down with it on the big truck. We got to Delhi and took it off the truck at the garage. The man reached in back and touched a wire . . . and the car started.

Just a silly old man. What does he know about cars?

Ah, so

If you have invested in anything, demanding that it not change when you know full well that all things change – your income, or your health, or your body, or the love of friends, or your life, or whatever – If you are holding onto non-change in a changing environment, you are going to be freaked out of your skull. You may cover it a thousand ways, but you are constantly frightened and running scared.

There's no way not to be in a universe in which all form is changing. The minute you try to hold anything back, it's like trying to hold back the waters of a raging river. You finally open to the flow, and from moment to moment it is: Ahhh . . . ooooo . . . oh . . . yeesh . . . ummm . . . yes.

There's a monk, who's in the monastery. A girl gets pregnant in the village and she doesn't want to say it's the fisherman, so she says it was the monk. When the baby comes, they take a torch light and they go up and knock on the monastery gate, and they say to the monk, "This is your baby. You raise it!"

And the monk says, "Ah, so." Takes the baby, closes the gate.

Nine years later the girl is dying. She doesn't want to die without confessing. She tells the truth: it was the fisherman. The village folk feel terrible. They all go up and knock on the monastery gate. The monk comes with a little boy, holding hands. They say, "We have to tell you we're terribly sorry. It wasn't your son. We will take over the rearing of this boy."

And the monk says, "Ah, so."

Hold on tightly, let go lightly. Ah, so.

Third Avenue Bus Driver

I once did a series of lectures in New York at the Sculpture Studio uptown. Every night I'd get on the Third Avenue bus to go uptown at rush hour. I did it for many days, and after a while I found that there was a certain bus driver who was driving at a certain time. I'd get on his bus, and all he was doing was the same thing every other bus driver was doing, but there was a quality in the way he was doing it that fed me when I got on that bus. Just a quality of his being, just in the way he looked at the meter, or drove the bus, or dealt with the traffic, or dealt with the people getting on the bus. He wasn't necessarily cheery, he wasn't necessarily telling jokes; he just flowed. He used different things at different times, but there was a quality of his being.

If Buddha came to New York City, how would he come? Why not as a driver on the Third Avenue bus? What better way to really be in contact with people?

The Family Brings Me Down

Whatever your method, does it allow you to cultivate this other quality of your being?

See, I thought for all those years that all I wanted was to get high, and I didn't want to come down. Then I figured out that I didn't want to be high, I wanted to be free! And if I wanted to be free, it meant I couldn't stand anywhere. Because if I was trying to hold onto my high, what happened was I'd say, "I can't go there. It brings me down."

Like I'd get so high, I'd be a combination of the Buddha and the heart of Christ. I'd be a walking statement of spiritual loveliness. And then I'd go home to see the family. Dad would say, "Got a job?" and I'd come crashing down! He'd do me in. Your parents know how to get you because they trained you. They know where your last stash of mind is.

I'd say, "Family brings me down. Can't be here. I can't go to the city, it brings me down. Don't want to leave the ashram, it brings me down."

Pretty soon, everything brought me down. It's attachment of mind. The game is to come and to go, and to learn finally how to be, as Christ said, "in the world but not of the world." Or as Don Juan talks about, how to be an impeccable warrior with controlled folly. How to live on the earth plane delightedly, and use the form as the vehicle of always coming into the formless through the form.

Meditation is a form; devotional yoga is a form. Why isn't standing in line a form? Why isn't doing your laundry a form? Why isn't paying your taxes, and changing your oil, and remembering your zip code – why aren't they forms for coming into liberation? Why are they entrapping? Why can't you convert them?

If you understand enough about where you're going, everything becomes a vehicle through which you get free.

Chip Off the Old Block

A woman comes to me and says, "My daughter ran away. She forged checks, she's so terrible." She does about a 15-minute monologue. She finishes, and I'm just sitting there, breathing in my nose . . . breathing out my nose . . . I'm right here for her; I'm listening to every word. I could repeat the whole story to her, my heart is open, I love her incredibly. But she's come to me and my job is not to get caught in her melodrama, to love her but not to buy her whole shtick.

So she finishes, and I'm right here, but she didn't get what she wanted. She wanted me to say, "Oh, God! You poor dear! Isn't that daughter an ungrateful wretch!"

I just said, "Right. Well, here we are."

She said, "No, you don't understand!!" And she did the whole thing again. It took about ten minutes this time. When she finished, I was still there, and she was still there.

Then something happened, and she laughed and said, "You know, she's really a chip off the old block. I was pretty wild myself when I was young."

I didn't demand that she come out of her drama, but I didn't keep her sucked into it. I don't have to live out her karma – she's having fun doing that. I merely have to create a space in which she is free to awaken, if she is in an evolutionary position where she is ready to do so.

A Nine-Day Fast

Somebody comes to me and says, "I'd like to fast."

I say, "Fine, why don't you do a nine-day fast?"

"Well, I'd only thought of doing a four-day fast."

"No, do a nine-day one. You want to fast, that's really good. It'll clean up your act."

"Well, what should I drink?"

"Oh, you can drink Mu tea." (I mean, you can say anything to anybody. You can tell them to stand on their head. It'll all get you there if you do it for the right reason.)

So the person comes in after seven days and says, "I haven't eaten in seven days."

Usually, if you're a teacher (with most of us at the level we're all playing), you give ego-boosts. So you say, "Pretty good. You're doing very well. Two more days, you'll be enlightened."

Then you walk outside and somebody comes up to you on the street and says, "Hey, man. You got a quarter? Geez, I haven't eaten in seven days."

Are you going to say, "Good! You're doing fine! Two more days, you'll be enlightened?"

You can feel the situation. In one case you encourage the person to keep not eating. In the other case, you give the quarter.

Meher Baba in Santa Fe

There are stages of development where you are fully conscious of the laws unfolding in front of you, so that you know, "When I do this, this will happen." You don't change it as a result; you're merely a viewer of how it all happened.

For me, at this point, it's more like a surprise. Like I'll be invited to give a lecture in some small town somewhere, and I won't know why I accepted that particular one. I go and I speak to the audience, and they don't seem particularly interested in what I have to say. I think, "What the hell am I doing here? Maharajji, what do you have in mind? What kind of nonsense is this?"

Then I stay overnight, and I'm left alone. I go from the motel by taxi to the airport. I've got a half an hour before the plane and I go in to have a cup of coffee. I sit down and somebody comes over and says, "May I share this table?"

"Certainly, sit down."

We look at each other and there it is! In that moment is, Oh, far out! That's what I'm doing in this town!

It's like when Meher Baba was crossing the United States by train. He got to Santa Fe and he got off the train. He walked into the town, and walked through the town, and walked up to a certain corner of the street. There was an old Indian standing there and he walked up to him. They looked at each other for a couple of seconds, then Meher Baba turned, walked back, got on the train and left.

He said, "Well, now my work is finished."

Changing Lenses

I really worked for a number of years at getting high and not coming down. And I learned a lot of different techniques for getting high by changing the lenses through which I see the world.

If you put on lens 1 and look up here, you see a 55-year-old, balding, attractive-looking gentleman. That's the physical plane – the plane where lust is, where you just see physical bodies. When you lust, you see everybody in terms of physical bodies – as a potential, a competitor, or irrelevant. As I've gotten older, it's interesting – I'm sure there are streets in Worcester where that lens is worn. I can walk down that street and be totally irrelevant now, like a walking lamppost.

Lens 2 is the psychosocial lens. That's the lens of personality and social role – of mothers, fathers, lawyers, doctors, social workers, students, seekers after the light, meditators, all the social roles. And all the psychological stuff of the Minnesota Multiphasic Personality Inventory: happy, and sad, and depressed. You look up here and you see a warm, charming lecturer, a mild manic-depressive.

You put on lens 3 and you see our mythic identities. You see Jung's archetypes; you see the kind of bigger-than-life roles we're playing. There's the Divine Mother. There's the Seeker After the Holy Grail. There's the Pillar of Society. You see all the archetypal roles. You also see, when you look up here, that I'm an Aries, which explains everything to those of you who are wearing lens number three.

Now lenses 1, 2 and 3 all describe individual differences among us. They peg how you're different from me, and how I'm different from her and from him. They're all lesser and greater and different from each other.

But if you put on lens 4 and you look into the eyes of another being, you meet another awareness, another being looking back at you. It's like looking through one of those glass windows: Are you in there? I'm in here. How did you get into that one? And what you see is another being in a space suit that involves lenses 1, 2 and 3 – that involves the physical body, the psychosocial identities, and the mythic or astral levels. You see what the Christians call a "fellow soul." You see another awareness. You see a fellow witness of the scene.

If you put on another lens, lens 5, you look and you see yourself looking at yourself looking at yourself. There's only one of us. Because if you get down into the smallest units of matter – the quarks and things like electrons and sub-neutrinos, all that stuff way down there behind the patterning of stuff – it's all the same stuff. It's all homogeneous and moves in and out of everything. There's only one of it. You can call it the One in the spiritual unity that lies behind the diversity. You can call it God if you want to. There's no name for it, and many names.

Put on yet one more lens and you disappear, and I disappear, and the lens disappears, and it all disappears. That's the other side of the One. That's the formless unmanifest, before it manifests into anything, into stuff. That's the state between thoughts. It's the one that keeps the Buddhists all happy.

Now it's interesting. When I say that I touched something, it meant that I came up and I met my soul, and I met the way in which I was a part of the universe. I was no longer needing to be special, because I was no longer so caught in my puny separateness that had to keep proving I was something. I was part of the universe, like a tree is, or like grass is, or like water is. Like storms, like roses. I was just part of it all. I had my unique function to play. I could see from there that everything had a unique form – it was all just lawfully playing with each other. All forms were related lawfully, I could see which "me" in form was part of the law. Nothing more, nothing less. It was no big deal, and yet it was very precious.

Out of My Mind

I had an interesting experience not long ago. I was in New Mexico, and I was asked to see a fellow who had a very advanced case of multiple sclerosis. He had no use of the lower part of his body, and he dragged around this little sort of hovel he lived in. His name was Juan. And I went to see Juan.

I've got to admit that the way I get caught is I get caught down on Channel 2 when somebody calls me and says, "Would you see this fellow? He's got MS and maybe you can help him." See, that sucks me in. And then I go to help him, which is the trap of righteousness: "Well, I'll help him." Like, "I'm good. I'll help him. I'll help Juan because he's got MS." Okay, that's the model in my head. Can you hear it?

So I walk in and he's squatting on the toilet. I sit down on the edge of the tub, and I'm about to look up – I'm sort of getting myself ready to help Juan who's got multiple sclerosis, right? That's where my head is. I look up, and I look into the eyes of a being who's not busy having multiple sclerosis. He's just another being. And it surprises me. Like, "What are you doing here? I came to see somebody with MS." He's just sitting there, looking at me. And it blows me away! I mean, I just … aaahhhh! It awakens me.

I grab him, and we're hugging and kissing, and we go into an hour of ecstasy. We're talking about the beauty of the universe and how exquisite it all is – the awesome nature of the way it works, including suffering, including MS, including death and what happens after death – and we're asking each other questions and marveling at it all.

When I leave him I think, Boy, did he help me! See, he got me and he pulled me just by his being. He didn't demand that I not be a helper, but he was there and, the minute I saw it, he drew me out of my mind into the present moment.

Frisbee

I was at Stinson Beach, at one of the nude beaches, several years back. (You don't have to visualize this if you don't want to.) I had been playing in the clay banks; we were all covered with clay. I had a Frisbee, I was running naked in the sunshine, water sparkling in the distance, my MG up on the hill. I mean it was perfect, all of it. It was essence.

I was about to throw the Frisbee when a memory went through my mind of the inscription over Gandhi's tomb, which says, "Think of the poorest person you've ever known, and ask whether your next act will be of any use."

Do you throw the Frisbee, or don't you? And that is part of the issue of what people in an affluent culture face.

I threw the Frisbee. And I continue to throw the Frisbee. Because I think my unique dharma is the balance of all this. It's the appreciation of the incredible bounty of the world I've been handed – this kind of royal life I've got – and, at the same moment, doing what I do to relieve suffering, without being drowned by the immensity of it.

A Deeper Connection

When you consider that somebody could push a button that would start a sequence of events in which 600 million to a billion people would die, including themselves, in order to be right – doesn't something seem wrong about that? Something seems wrong to me.

We started out with the "just war" concept, which snuck in after Constantine bought out the Christians (before that the Christians were all Quaker-like) and meant that you could kill somebody who was going to kill you, but you didn't kill women and children and old people – non-combatants. Then in the Second World War – sometime around when we started to bomb Hamburg – we sort of bought into Hitler's philosophy: you just kill them all. Even before the nuclear bomb, we were firebombing. Like we firebombed Tokyo one day; we learned how to drop firebombs all around the periphery of an area, and that creates a vacuum so that the fire rushes in and burns everything. We killed more people in one day in Tokyo, before the atomic bomb, than we did in Hiroshima. So we had already let go of the concept of a "just war" a long time ago.

But you never think about the way you are sort of quietly acquiescing to a whole trip until it becomes apparent. Dan Ellsberg regales me with facts that chill my blood – like every President since Truman used the threat of first strike as a political playing card in international relations. All the time we're saying, "We wouldn't use first strike!" Or like a B-52 bomber that dropped a nuclear bomb by error over Greensboro, North Carolina. It was one of those bombs that's a thousand times more powerful than the one that went off at Hiroshima (the kind that was used at Hiroshima is now used as a trigger for the new bombs), and five of the six fail-safe mechanisms failed on that bomb. If one more had failed, North Carolina would have been unusable for 24,000 years.

Aren't those interesting facts? And you just keep adding one after the other after the other after the other until something in you says, "Hey, something isn't right here!" Our rational minds have just gotten off the wall a little bit with their delight in paranoia: "We're gonna protect ourselves against them!"

As I traveled around, what I saw in city after city was this intuitive sense in people that something isn't right. Not out of "ought" or "should" or even fear or urgency, although that's all part of it. But even when you're not caught in your separateness, even when you're really spacious, there is still an intuitive sense of the harmony of the universe that leads you to act in certain ways. You don't do it because you're righteous, you don't do it because somebody's going to give you points, you don't do it because you're angry, and you don't even do it because you're afraid.

There's a good part of me that's saying, "Well, the world may blow up. Ah, so. That'll be interesting." But there's another part that's saying, "Oh, the children! My God, we can't do that!" You begin to see there's no way you can NOT act when you're in a form. You vote, whether you vote or not. Reagan, in 1980, won a landslide victory: 52% of the 29% of registered voters bothered to vote – and the registered voters are 50% of the eligible voters. It means he won by about two votes. You don't vote, you vote. There's no way not to act.

What I sense in all of that is an intuitive way of acting – acting from a deeper part of our beings, an acting in which we start to trust ourselves, a way in which we meet in the intuitive heart instead of in the intellect. A deeper place of connection.

Peace Day

I was best man at a wedding in a church in Tiburon, and I got very high before the ceremony on some friendly chemical from somebody. I had the rings in my pocket. The minister started to talk about God reaching out to humanity, and I went out to the place he was talking about. The next thing I knew, the rabbi and the groom were shaking me to get the rings!

Well, in that state, when I met the minister I said, "You know, I've always wanted to give a sermon in a church, but nobody ever invites me."

He said, "I'm inviting you."

I said, "I accept."

So it turned out that I was going to give a sermon in the middle of my vacation. On the morning of the sermon, I got up out of my carnal bed and got in my car to go to the church to "be Ram Dass" – except it was Dick Alpert, and Ram Dass wasn't anywhere in sight! I intoned mantras, and I looked at pictures, and I said, "These people have asked for Ram Dass, you get here!" But still, not a thing happened. So I got to the church – and they were all nice people: sort of middle-class New Age. I muddled through; I ran old tapes.

Now it turned out that that day was "Peace Day" at the church. There were some Buddhist monks there that were part of a sect that was walking for peace around the world. This group was walking from San Diego to Seattle, and they'd stopped at that church that morning. That afternoon they were going to walk across the Golden Gate Bridge, for peace. After the ceremony, as I was leaving, people said to me, "Are you going to join the walk?" Now I had been up until about five the night before (it was Saturday night, and you can't be busy living Sunday morning when you're in the middle of Saturday night), so I'd been waiting to finish the service and stagger back to bed. I said, "Well, I'm afraid I have other plans . . ."

I said goodbye to everybody, left the church, got into the car, drove back across the bridge, all the way to the house. I went upstairs – and I knew somehow: I want to walk across that bridge. I thought, Isn't it funny? I've never walked across the Golden Gate Bridge. Here not only can I walk across it, but I can also do it for peace. What a fantastic thing.

So I washed my face, and turned around and went back out and drove back across the bridge, and arrived back at the church just as the march was starting out. I went into the crowd and walked along. It was this beautiful, warm, sunny day. You know how San Francisco has that white hill, magic city look, and the sailboats were all out in the Bay. The people I was marching with were all ages, all different kinds of people. Not the kind of people I was usually seeing at a gathering. There was a gentleness about the people, a softness. We were all waving; cars were blowing their horns as they went by us across the bridge.

There was a moment, in the middle of the bridge, when I experienced a feeling that I was in exactly the right place at the right moment, a feeling of Yeah! Ah! It was a place in which my human-ness and my divinity somehow clicked in together, and there was a fullness of the moment, enough-ness, what it is.

What interested me was that at that moment I was a cipher. I was another one of the crowd. But I knew I was part of the reawakening or the expression of the intuitive heart/mind of humanity, saying, "Something isn't right. I've got to stand up and count myself in."

The Salt March

There was a time when Mahatma Gandhi was a sort of senior advisor to the Congress Party in India. The English had become extremely oppressive to the Indians, with a lot of unfair and unjust laws. The Indians finally realized they just had to get rid of the British, the most powerful nation in the world.

The Congress Party came to Gandhi and said, "Would you help us? What do you suggest we do?"

He said, "I don't know. I'll have to meditate on it."

He went into meditation, and after a week they came and they said, "Well, Mahatmaji, what do we do?"

He said, "I don't know. I'm still meditating on it."

A month and a half later they were all totally freaked because politicians want to have an action to take. He kept stalling and stalling, saying, "I haven't heard the message yet." Because, as the Tao says, "The truth waits for eyes unclouded by longing." As long as you're busy trying to get rid of the British, you're not going to hear it.

Finally he came out, and he said, "I heard it." And he started walking towards the ocean.

The British had imposed a salt tax on the Indian people, which meant that they had to buy salt from a British company, even though salt was readily available in India. Each Indian family had to spend up to two weeks of their income for salt a year because it's a hot country and they need the salt.

Mahatma Gandhi started marching with his followers, about 70 people, towards the ocean. Pretty soon more and more people joined them, and people were lining the path. Many, many days it took – frail little man with a cane, walking gently. He finally got to the ocean. He went in the ocean and took his bath of purification in the Mother. Then he walked up on the shore, reached down, and picked up a handful of salt, which God had deposited on the ocean's edge. He was breaking the British law; he was mining his own salt.

And that one act of picking up a handful of salt . . . Within a month, 60,000 Indians had been imprisoned for mining their own salt. That single act was the major turning point in breaking the back of the British rule – the most powerful country in the world. One scrawny old man reached down and picked up one handful of salt. It touched something in people that was so deep in what is real for them that their hearts could open, and they could go with it.

Where You Sit

Dan Ellsberg and I were talking about Allen Ginsberg, who was sitting on the railway tracks at Rocky Flats in meditation, and got arrested. Those tracks are where the trains come out of Rocky Flats, and they bring out all the nuclear waste material that the plant keeps exuding. That plant makes all the triggers for the new bombs and the stuff that regenerates the old bombs (because they keep losing their potency). So if you stop the excreta of that one plant, nothing new can happen. There's an automatic freeze. And pretty soon all the old ones lose their power. So it's a very good place to sit!

Now meditators always say, "It's important that you sit."

So Dan said to me, "You see? It proves it's not only important that you sit, it's also important where you sit."

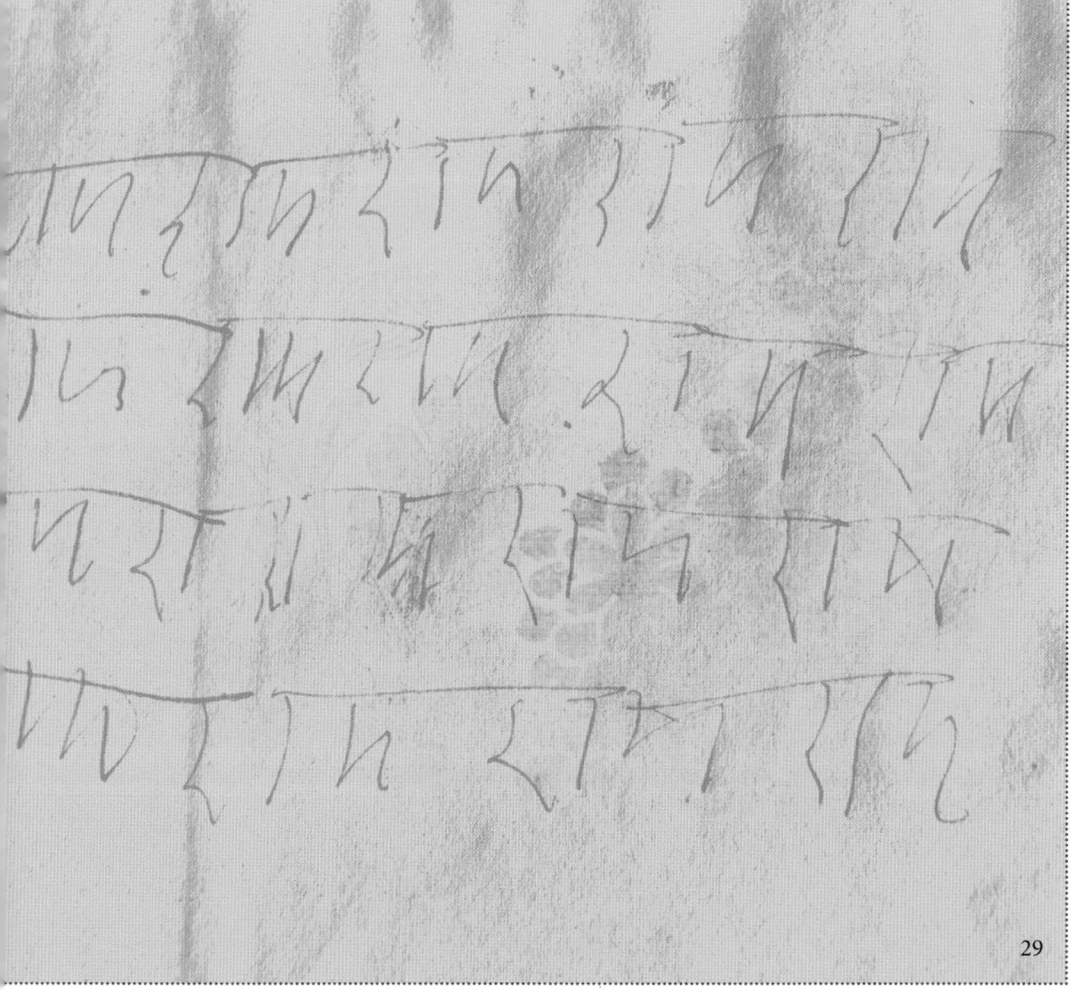

Everybody's Uncle Henry

I put out an album some years ago called "Love, Serve, Remember," which had readings from the Gospel of John, music, all kinds of neat things. It was a beautiful album, with a beautiful booklet with pictures, and the whole thing was a mail order item for $4.50. My father looked at it – and he's a very wealthy, conservative Republican, a capitalist, president of a railroad at that time – and he looks at this and he says, "Great job here! Gee, you know – $4.50? You could probably sell this in a store for $10, maybe $15."

I said, "Yeah, I know."

He said, "Would fewer people buy it?"

I said "No, same number."

He said, "Well, I don't understand you. If you can sell it for $10 and you're selling it for $4.50 . . . what's wrong, are you against capitalism or something?"

I tried to figure out how to explain to him what was going on for me. I said, "Dad, did you just try a law case for Uncle Henry?"

He said, "Yeah. And it was a damn tough case. I spent a lot of time in the law library."

I said, "You win it?"

He said, "Yeah, I won it."

Now my father is a very successful attorney, and he has charged fees that are commensurate with his reputation. So I said, "Well, I bet you charged him an arm and a leg for that one!" "What, are you out of your mind? That's Uncle Henry. I couldn't charge him!"

I said, "Well, that's my problem. If you can find me anybody that isn't Uncle Henry, I'll rip them off."

Let's just imagine that the only people left are family. What are we going to do? It changes the whole idea of advertising, of right livelihood, of how you live, how you treat other people, how you treat their suffering. How do you treat the suffering of family? Believe me, when somebody you love is suffering, it's worse than when you're suffering. You'd rather you suffer than they suffer. Do you feel that way about somebody in Africa? Somebody in Nepal? A homeless person here on the street of Worcester? How do you use your mind to protect yourself?

Ink Being Poured Into Water

I hang out with dying people because it gets me really high. I really think there's probably something weird about me; when I know I'm going to be with somebody dying, I get into ecstasy. Isn't that far out? It's like being with my guru, because you can't really be a phony in those situations. You've just got to be right there.

I'd like to describe for you a moment last December in Cambridge, with a gal named Jean Youmans. Jean had been ill with cancer for a long time. She was in a very, very late stage. She was in her bedroom at home with an oxygen tank, with nurses in constant attendance. She was a wonderful Quaker lady, who had taken up meditation about three years before, but had always been quietly listening for the "still small voice within," as the Quakers so beautifully do. I came back from India earlier than I'd expected, probably for this reason. Mary McClellan said, "Jean Youmans has been calling for you. She's very close to death." So I said, great, let's go over there.

Mary and Jean's husband took me upstairs to the room. I came in and said, "Hello, Jean." And they said, "We'll leave you two alone." They went out and closed the door… and there were Jean and I.

Jean was very frail, and very beautiful, and very weak. She said, "Ram Dass, I've finished my work. I want to die, and I want you to help me."

Now the predicament that I'm in is that my rational mind knows some stuff, but when the cards are down I really can't just use that, because I don't trust that enough. Usually when somebody asks me, or puts me in a position demanded by the purity of the way they are asking, or the purity of the moment, it throws me out of my thinking mind into a space in which whatever comes out, comes out. I have to trust that. Oftentimes things come out that sound like tremendous chutzpah – to me! (I'm giving you the two levels of the game here.)

So when Jean said that, I emptied my mind, and I heard myself say, "Jean, that all sounds like ego to me. How do you know your work is done? Maybe you're going to have to lose each sense, sense by sense. Don't rush it. Milk it for as much as you can. Do as much work as you can this life. Believe me, when your time is come, it'll be done. You don't have to engineer it, it's okay – just listen."

(That's like one woman who was dying, who said, "Well, tonight I'm going to die." She called her family, her friends, and they had a big party, and everybody said goodbye, and she went into her room. The next morning: "Oh my God, I'm still alive." This went on for, like, three weeks, and she kept saying goodbye, and goodbye, and goodbye, until she had finished being somebody saying goodbye, and then she could die.)

So Jean lay back and thought about that for awhile, and then she said to me, "But Ram Dass, I'm so bored." See?

"Well, Jean, that's because you're so busy dying."

Often I'll come into a room to visit somebody who I've been working with, and they'll be surrounded by family, and the whole situation is THE DRAMA. I'll say, "Oh, excuse me. I'll come back later. I see you're all busy dying." I mean, it's a very linear storyline: "I'm dying, I'm dying. I need water, I'm dying, I'm dying." You can be busy dying, but it gets boring after a while to be busy being somebody that's dying. It's like you can get a sports car and drive it, but after a while you'd like to get out. It's a boring scenario to play it on and on, but you don't have to. That's your mind.

I said, "Well, Jean, I would get bored too if I was busy dying for as long as you have. That's a very draggy role. All the time – Who are you? I'm dying. Dying is a thing to do, too; you don't have to buy into that very seductive melodrama."

So she reflected about that. (See, these moments of conversation are supposed to be very holy. And this flippancy, where does it come from? That's the sword, you know. I hope there's enough love behind it).

She said, "I've been having this vision, and in this vision there is a little boy sitting in a tree and there is an angry man walking around the bottom of the tree. I feel that that has something to do with my death, and so I have been sending the angry man golden light to make him less angry."

"Well Jean, that sounds like one of the ten thousand horrible visions and the ten thousand beautiful visions. If you're going to sit and screw around with every one of them, you're never gonna die." There are innocent little children and there are menacing men, and that's the way the universe is. Until you can say, "Ah, so" and just go through them, every one is just taking you on a little side trip.

Then she said, "Well, Ram Dass, it feels like everybody's pushing against me. When they come in, the energy is so overwhelming. When somebody walks, or talks, or the light, or the sound, or the senses – it's all too much."

"Well, Jean, the image I get when I hear you telling me that is the complaint of a one-quart container of water when a gallon of water is being poured into it. The problems seems to be the size of the container you think you are. As you get closer to death and your models are breaking down a little bit, you're starting to experience more energy and more of the universe, but the model of who you are is still so little and cramped that you're feeling overloaded by everything. Why don't you, instead of being busy being who you thought you were, allow yourself to open into the universe. Come on, we'll do it together, Jean. You hear the clock, Jean? Hear it ticking?"

"Yes."

"You become the clock. Take it inside yourself, so the clock is ticking within you. Hear the children playing outside? Bring them in. Inside. All within you. Keep expanding outward, let it all be within you. Take it all."

As I did this meditation, we started to expand outward until it got very spacious. The whole room turned luminous with purple light. Jean was lying back on her pillow, a look of total bliss on her face; she sat up, and she was radiant with light. She comes over and starts to stroke my face as if she is looking at a human being, at this phenomenon of a body, and she's tenderly stroking it. And I stroke her face. Then she kisses me. And I kiss her. And we hold each other. It's a moment that is absolutely perfect in its presence. It was like a celebration of form from the point of view of the formless.

I mean, even the little tiny thought forms in my head – Well, this is the next thing to necrophilia, and, Do you know her husband is downstairs? and, They're Quakers, what will they think of this? – all those little niggly-piggly things in my head were just like little lights around the edge. They didn't have much juice to them because the whole thing was simply what it was, and it was absolutely perfect. Then she lay back on the pillow, and we held hands for about 10 or 15 minutes.

I said, "Well, Jean, you understand everything I do. There's no more sense wasting time. Probably I won't see you again in this body, so stay conscious. Namaste." And I left.

I flew down to New York that night, and the next morning at seven I got a call; she'd died during the night. Her husband said, "Her dying was like ink being poured into water. It was just expanding outward. I came away from her death with one of the deepest experiences of peace I'd ever had in my life."

It's interesting that when it works, when a person stays conscious through that transition, if you're around them you end up feeling like you have been blessed. You feel you have experienced incredible grace from someone showing you the ephemeral nature of the body from a quiet space.

Behind the Veil

You get to appreciate the uniqueness of everybody. The people around you, you appreciate them. Not judge them, but appreciate them. Even the stinkers. You appreciate an essence stinker instead of, "You ought to not be a stinker." If a stinker gets to you, well, that's your work on yourself. Because they're just being who they are. You begin to give people space; you begin to appreciate the way in which God manifests in this multiplicity of exquisite forms.

For a long time on my puja table there was Buddha, there was Christ, there was Maharajji, and there was Caspar Weinberger (Reagan's Secretary of Defense). See? Because he was a symbol of the kind of person I had a hard time seeing God in. Because I got caught in his actions – and actions can be good or evil. Beings aren't good or evil, beings just are. You have to look behind the veil: Buddha, Christ, Maharajji, Caspar. Buddha – aaaah. Christ – aaaah. Casper – ugh. See? My heart closes.

And you watch your heart open and close until you learn what you're getting caught in, until you learn how to look through the veil.

Maharajji and the Yogi Medicine

Psychedelics showed me that the world wasn't the way I thought it was, and that I was stuck in my conceptual mind thinking about the world. I really wanted to find a way to stay in the place I tasted only on Saturday nights. I started a program where my life started to orient toward how to get high and stay high. I did everything that I could think of to do that. I was surrounded by some very good game players, like Alan Watts and Aldous Huxley and Gerald Herd and people like that. And it seemed like everybody was trying to learn to do that same thing.

By 1967, I saw I wasn't going to do it with chemicals; there might be a way to do it, but I didn't know how. Everybody I looked at – Allen Ginsberg, Bill Burroughs, all the people — we'd get high and then everybody came down. It was like a yo-yo: you'd go up and you'd come down and you'd go up and you'd come down. And you'd try different things. If I go up standing this way, facing east, doing this prayer, and take this much, under these conditions, after fasting in the desert . . . And I still came down. By '67 I knew I didn't know enough about all that to be able to stay in those states.

So I went to India and I met Neem Karoli Baba, and he said, "You use that yogi medicine?" I didn't understand, but it turned out the yogi medicine was LSD, so I said yes. He said, "Have you got any of it?" I said yes. This old man is sitting on a bench with a blanket, and I brought out my stash and gave him one pill, which was 300 micrograms of Owsley's White Lightning. He looked at it and said, "Give me some more," so I gave him two, which was 600, and he said, "Give me some more," so I gave him three, which was 900. And he took it. I thought, being a scientist, This is going to be very interesting! And nothing happened to him at all! That disturbed me, because that was our great medicine and nothing had happened; it was like he drank water. After I gave Maharajji LSD that first time, a devotee said to me, "Well, you know that's nothing. A couple of years ago a sadhu came to see Maharajji." Some sadhus take tiny bits of arsenic for devotional purposes; it's very good, gets you high. He had his two-year supply of arsenic, which was a lethal dose for about ten people. Maharajji said, "Where's your arsenic?"

"Oh, Maharajji, I don't have any arsenic!"

"Give me your arsenic."

Maharajji took the whole thing and ate it. Everybody started to cry . . . and nothing happened.

I came back to America and told everybody, but I had the lurking suspicion that maybe what he did, since he had so many powers, was he clouded my mind and threw it over his shoulder, and I just thought he put it in his mouth.

When I came back to India in 1971, I couldn't find him for a while. When I finally found him, he called me up to him one day and said, "Did you give me some medicine when you were here last time?"

"Yes."

"Did I take it?"

"Well, I thought so."

"Well, what happened?"

"Nothing."

"Oh. Jao, go."

Then he called me back and he said, "You got any more?"

I brought out what I had. There were five pills, one of which was broken. These were also 300 micrograms each. He didn't take the broken one, but he took the other four – that's 1200 micrograms – and he took each one and stuck it on his tongue like he wanted to make sure, because he knew my mind. I didn't tell him this, but he knew I had doubts.

When he finished taking it, he said, "Will it make me crazy?" I said probably. He said, "Can I take water?" I said yes. "Hot or cold?" Doesn't matter. So he got cold water, drank a glass. He said, "How long will it take?" I thought, well, he has a big body weight, and I'm calculating body weight, 1200 mics . . . I figured I'd play it absolutely safe, so I said an hour. I figured that would cover all eventualities.

He called an old sadhu over who had this big watch, and he was sitting there with this watch. At one point Maharajji went under his blanket and then came out looking absolutely mad! I thought, "Oh, my God! What have I done to this poor man! You know, he's an old man and he thought these were vitamins or something, and he probably threw it over his shoulder last time and . . . What have I done?"

He just laughed at me. Nothing happened to him at all.

As I understand it now, when you're in Detroit you don't have to take a bus to Detroit. We are busy being someplace and we take it to go someplace else. But if you are the someplace else as well, it's like water.

When he got all done, he said, "Yes. These medicines were known thousands of years ago. But most of that knowledge has been lost. Yogis used them in the past, but they used them with fasting and diets and so on." He said, "It's useful. It allows you to come in and have the darshan of Christ, but you can only stay two hours and then you have to leave."

I said, "Yeah. That's what I thought, too."

He said, "It's not the real samadhi."

So later I said to him, "Should I use it anymore?"

He said, "Sure. If you're in a cool place, and you're alone, and you're feeling much peace, and your mind is turned toward God, it could be useful."

I've sort of followed that, more or less.

Tony's Mahasamadhi

While I was staying in the cabin at my father's farm in New Hampshire, this young fellow Tony came to visit me. He had been living down on the Lower East Side in New York, and he came to say that he would like to study yoga with me. Now I had just been in India, doing raja yoga for six or eight months, and so I said sure. I don't even know how he found me, but he did.

His folks had a place up in Winnipesaukee, and he'd go there and come see me every week, and I taught him. After a couple of months I'd taught him everything I knew, and he was already doing everything better than I could. So by the fall I said to him, "Look, I think I've gone as far as I can go with you; you'd better find a real teacher." I gave him a list of what he could do, or he could go to India and all.

He said "No, I think I know the rudimentary stuff. I'm gonna go into a cave on my parents' ranch in Arizona and spend the winter there doing this. All I want to know is could I check in with you every month or so?"

Sure.

So every month he'd fly to wherever I was. I'd see that he was a yogi, and we'd talk, and then he'd go back to his cave. He looked like a different human being; he was turning into this in-credible yogi, a very beautiful, beautiful man.

Then came the spring, and he didn't show up any more. I finally got a letter from his mother saying, "I know you'll be happy to know my son has completed his work. He has entered ma-hasamadhi," which means enlightenment, the great samadhi, the final liberation. That seemed unbelievable to me! First of all, that any student of mine could be entering mahasamadhi. And then, why should it be a student? Why not me? So I had certain doubts about it, but I didn't say anything. She said, "I'd like to come and see you and bring you his diary."

So she came to New Hampshire and had his diary with her. He had been found in his cave; blood had come from his nose and was on the wall of the cave. His heart had burst and he had died from that. In his diary, the last message read: "Dear Mother: Tell Ram Dass I have completed my work. I am one with Christ and Maharajji. You need not worry, I am watching over you always. Via con dios, Tommy."

Now the thing was that that message was written in a scrawl – big words, just a few words on a page. The minute I saw it, it reminded me of those moments when I would have a very heavy acid trip, and right at the highest moment I would get the word that was the key to the universe. For the good of humanity, I would go across the floor on hands and knees for a pencil to write the word, so I didn't have to spend the rest of the time remembering it (because it was so pro-found). The next day it would turn out to be "IS" or something like that. So I looked at those words and I thought he had written that message while he was on acid.

She said to me, "My son reached mahasamadhi."

I said, "Well, I really don't know. How would I know? But I know somebody who knows." See, because the way you know what you know is either you've had an experience of it, which is your senses, which of course may be wrong anyway, or you know somebody who knows and you ask him. Or you extrapolate from what you know to what you don't know, and it seems reasonable. In this case I said, "Well, I don't know, but I know who knows. Why don't you give me a picture of your son and when I'm in India next time I'll show him the picture."

She gave me Tony's high school graduation picture (which looked just like every high school graduation picture you've ever seen), and I put it in my bag. A year and several months later, I'm in India, sitting with a group of Western devotees around Maharajji, and he's going through everybody's wallet and looking at pictures and saying, "Ma, Ma," and all these kinds of things. A very intimate moment. I remember that I've got this picture back in my duffel bag. So I go running across the courtyard. I get this picture, which I've had sitting there for a year now. I walk in and hand it to Maharajji.

Now before I tell you the rest of the story, I've got to add in another incident. Two weeks after the mother came to see me, Tony's younger brother came to see me and said, "I've got to tell somebody this. I went to visit my brother with a friend the day he died, and we took some acid together." I thought, Aha! I knew it! It wasn't mahasamadhi – the kid took acid!

He continued, "Then we went swimming, and we were very, very high. My brother came over to me and went to embrace me. I was paranoid and went into a homosexual panic and pushed him away. He got frightened and told us to leave. That was the last we ever saw of him."

Now, hear that story. In my mind what I see is him walking back to his room, being caught, very unhappy, wanting to get out and go. He decides to do his pranayam, or his breath control, and has the acid in him, which overrides the limitations of his system, and he bursts his heart in some way and dies. It's an act of will, a suicide in that sense. I mean, that's not necessarily disadvantageous, but it's hardly mahasamadhi material.

Okay, now you've got it. I hand Maharajji the picture, and he looks at Tony's picture and he says, "Oh, he's dead." Yes. He said, "He died from that medicine."

I said, "Yeah. That's what I thought." You see, in my mind: Drugs! I mean, you think I would be free of that, but . . .

And he says, "Oh, no, no. He finished his work. He wanted you to know he had finished his work. And his mother should know he'll watch over her all the time." Line for line, everything Tony had written.

I said, "Well, Maharajji, how could he have finished his work if he died that way?" He looked at me like, no, he finished his work. I realized, at that moment, that when you're done, the hook comes out from the wings. How you go off is just how you go off; it's not that big a deal. It's sort of how conscious you stay through it, not which dramatic exit line you have.

The Divine Mother

When I was in the temple in India, my guru pointed to all the beautiful, beautiful Indian women who were sitting around him, feeding him. My guru eats about 15 meals a day, and these women cook all night. To cook for a high being is such high spiritual work, and he just keeps eating all day. A spoonful of this comes in and then a spoonful of that. He's doing their work for them. He's taking on their karma.

He pointed to the women and said to me, "Who are these women?"

I looked and said, "They are beautiful Indian women."

"Nay. Who are these women?"

"Well," I said, "They are all your loving devotees."

"Nay, nay! Who are these women?"

"I give up. Who are these women?"

He said, "Ma. Ma." The Divine Mother. They're all the Divine Mother. So I absorbed that for a while. I looked at each of these women as my mother, which was pretty interesting as that certainly changes your "take" on women.

Then he points to the sadhus – the men sitting around – and he says, "Who are they?"
Now I'm not even trying. I say, "I don't know."

He says, "Ma." They're the Divine Mother too. All the Divine Mother. Maya. The illusion.

Morphine and Mescaline

I remember going to the hospital to visit my mother when she was dying. She was on morphine, and I was on mescaline (or something like that). We sat together, and we became these two floating souls, watching the death of this body. We entered into a space of love, where there was no more "mother-ness" and "child-ness." It was there, but it wasn't the heavy drama that we were both stuck in all the time. We met in the space of, "Are you here? I'm here." The space where there was no birth and there was no death. There was no drama going down, just shared awareness. It was quite luminous, and she was laughing.

The next day when I came in, she was off the morphine. I said, "Wasn't that a great day we had yesterday?"

She said, "It was terrible! They gave me drugs and I was out of my mind." She couldn't accept what that moment had been because it was so discontinuous with her normal waking consciousness, with her model of how reality was, that she would rather reject her actual experience than question the reality that she had built as a total field.

The Cat and the Lizard

I remember once I was down at Big Sur. I had been given a house down there near Esalen, and it came with a cat. In the morning I'd be meditating, and the cat would come in with its prey that it was going to eat. It loved me, so it would come over and sit between my legs and eat the lizard, or whatever it was. The lizard would be alive and flapping, and I'd be sitting there meditating. I'd feel bad for the lizard, and then I'd hate the cat. But a moment before I had loved the cat.

Who should I hate and who should I love?

I saw that my judging mind was just my judging mind, and this was the process of the universe. Was I really ready to decide that I was to judge whether the cat was bad for eating the lizard? I saw that I had to stretch further than that.

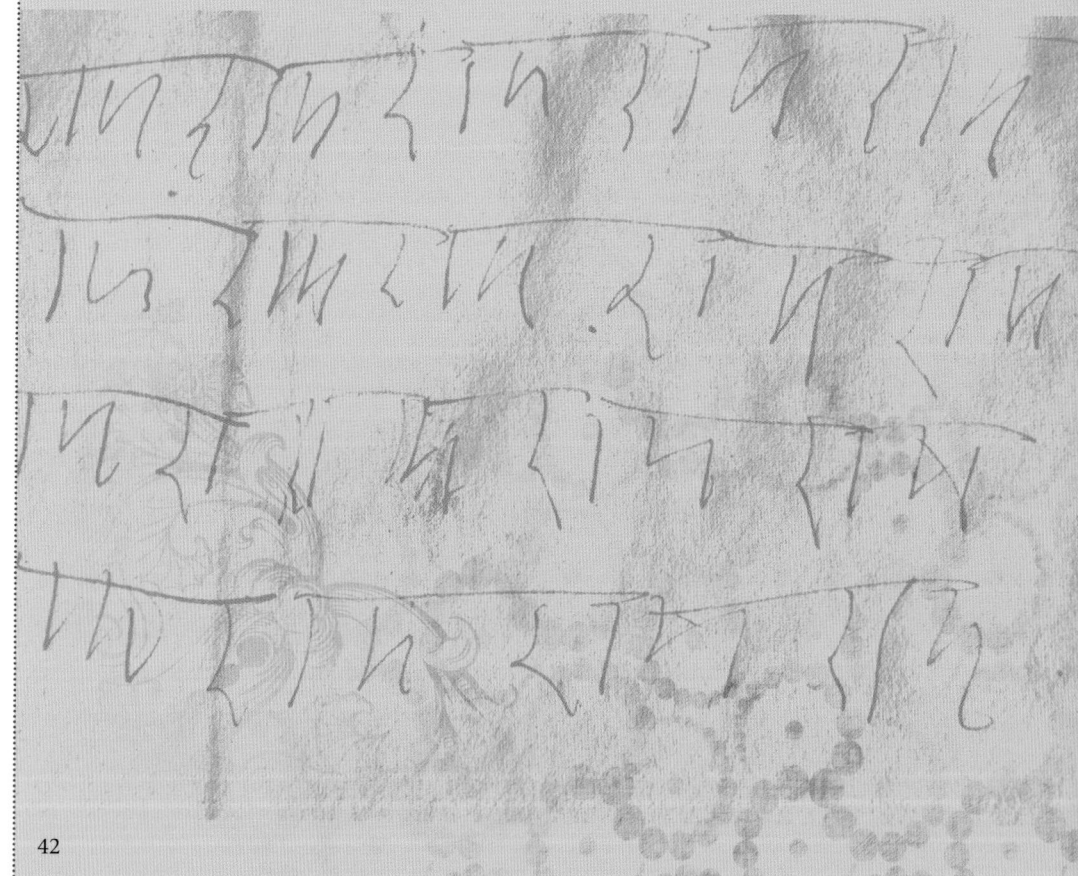

42

Roast Beef and Chapatis

When I came back from India in '68, I moved into the cabin behind my father's house. My father had this big estate, and I lived in this little cabin. I would cook my own food every day, and I would cook the same food every day. It was lentils and rice, plus I made my chapatis with flour and water. I was going to live as a yogi. I bathed out of a bucket, which is what I had been doing in India. I was going to hold onto my high no matter what.

And there, a hundred feet away, was this huge house, with smells of roast beef pouring out of it. I could hear the television, and music playing out over his golf course. I was sitting there, cooking my little pot of kedgeree, and feeling very righteous. Oh, was I righteous! Oh, boy!

Then I saw how much I was preoccupied with those issues – that I was doing the reverse twist of that whole game. If we're going to be free, we're going to be free about the preoccupation with our worldly conditions. It doesn't mean we won't notice them, it doesn't mean we won't try to optimize them. The question is: how much emotional, attached mind are we investing in optimizing them?

Shaktipat

At one point I was traveling around the world with Swami Muktananda, who had this capacity to give shaktipat – direct energy. I've sat in a room where Muktananda is just gently playing his ektara, and suddenly somebody gets up and starts dancing. This is somebody who didn't expect to dance — a rotund gentleman in a dark blue serge suit in Melbourne, Australia – and he gets up and starts to do incredible Indian dancing. The man next to him, who looks just like a professor in a tweed jacket and a pipe, starts to do mudras – exquisite, perfect mudras – but the look on his face is one of total perplexity. Somebody else is doing automatic breathing and bouncing across the floor. The whole place begins to look like the ward of a mental hospital, and Swami Muktananda's just sitting up there with his eyes closed, playing his ektara.

What is happening is that he is like a beam of energy, and he's activating the kundalini – the energy in people. It's called "giving shakti." The energy starts to come up in the person, and wherever a center is blocked – let's say it gets up to the second center or the third center and can't get any further – it comes out in a certain behavioral manifestation. If a little of it gets blocked at one point and more at another, then there's a different manifestation. There's a chart of the centers and the 26 manifestations (or whatever it is), and they're all very straightforward: This one will dance, that one will do breathing, another one will pass out, whatever. He passes out the dittoed sheets, and you can keep score of who's got which chakra-thing.

What happens is the energy is like water going up a tube that comes to a crimp in the tube; because of the pressure it's got to go out. People working with energies attempt to open their chakras by forcing against that blockage. Psychedelics do a similar process of forcing, or over-riding, existing structures. It's a fallacy to think of the chakras and the sushumna as physical things; they're really astral entities, not nerves you could dissect in anatomy. And when you're working within these energy systems, you might be given a certain mantra, a bij sound, for opening a certain chakra. It's given by a diagnostician. Or you might be given a visualization, like a mandala in Tibetan work.

What You See on Main Street

You and I are seeing different things. We're seeing our own creations. I can show you that even as a psychologist. If I take a group of people who are hungry and I run through a town with them, at the end of the town I ask them, "What did you see?"

They say, "I saw Dunkin' Donuts and the pizza parlor."

I take somebody who's got a rattle in their engine and they're worried about it, and on the other side of town I say, "What did you see?"

They say, "I saw garages and service stations."

You take somebody that's horny and you run them through the town. At the end, as you can predict, they saw that person standing on the corner under the clock, they didn't see pizza parlors or service stations.

Desire manifests in perception. It's perceptual selectivity. You actually pick out of the infinite stimulation that is occurring to your senses all the time, in every sense dimension, which fits into your model of how you think it ought to be, and those models come along with attachment. Desires are at the root of them and your identifications. "I am hungry" – and the universe turns into what is edible and what is not edible.

Roommates

I was taking a meditation course once, and I arrived five minutes after the course began. You go in silence, you're not allowed to talk to anyone else during the course. I had a roommate, and he was very neat; he did hospital corners on his bed. I decided he didn't like me – that I was a slob and he didn't like me. I spent all week staying out of the room because I felt he didn't like me. I figured I might snore, maybe that was it. But I just got a feeling that he was so clean and neat that he couldn't like somebody like me. I built up this incredible feeling that this guy hated me.

When the course was over, he walked up to me and said, "I want to introduce myself and tell you that just knowing I was in the same room with you and sharing this with you helped my meditation so much. Thank you. I feel so much love for you, I wish I could have told you."

I suddenly saw my mind. I had created this incredible mountain of paranoia and spent a whole week worrying about it. And it was all in my mind.

Trungpa Teaches Don Juan

Trungpa Rinpoche was teaching this weekend course on Don Juan up in Barnett, Vermont. I went to the lecture and sat in the back, wearing shorts and a T-shirt. I was just driving through to Canada, and they said I could come in as a guest.

Trungpa came in and spoke for about 20 minutes. I mean, here these people had come for hundreds of miles and he speaks for 20 minutes, which is chutzpah to begin with. Then he says, "Are there any questions?"

Somebody asks a question and Rinpoche says, "Why doesn't Ram Dass answer that?" I think to myself, He's getting paid. Why shouldn't he answer it?

Everybody turns around, "Oh, Ram Dass is here, yeah, yeah. Ram Dass come up . . ." Well, it's all show biz. Sure. I come up and he's sitting in a chair, and next to him is a pot with goldenrod in it, which I happen to be allergic to, and there's a microphone with a low stand. I'm tall. I have to kneel on the stand with my head through the goldenrod and speak into the microphone. Which I do – you know, if you're going to play . . . I do it, and give a very erudite answer.

I get up and start to walk back, and the next question comes and Trungpa says, "Why doesn't Ram Dass answer that question?" So I come up again and I play the scholar, and I'm talking about kundalini and sushumnas, and I suddenly realize what he's doing to me. In this weekend on Don Juan he has just re-created a situation in which I am cast as Castaneda. Here I am, this intellect, this ex-professor, giving answers at the flick of this guy's finger, being this bumbling fool, and he's just playing with me. It blew me away; it was so exquisite.

I got up and walked over to Trungpa and touched his feet. I explained to the group what had happened, what I'd just appreciated. He was giving them an essence teaching about Don Juan. He was showing it to them, not just talking about it.

Joe and Rosie

I have had some strange teachers because I'm open to teachings wherever I can get them. Let me tell you about two of my teachers.

I have these friends, John and Toni Lilly, who have been working with dolphins for many years, and they asked me if I'd like to swim with the dolphins. I said I'd love to. So I went with a friend of mine to these huge tanks where Joe and Rosie, these two dolphins, were. My friend went into the pool, and I watched the dolphins with my friend for a little while, and then I got into the pool, and pushed off from the edge and started swimming. The dolphins went by me very fast. The first thing I was aware of was how big they were – I mean, these weren't little fish, these were big, big things. I was clearly in their territory. I didn't have my feet on the ground, and they were in control of the scene.

Then Joe came up, opened his mouth, and put it around my wrist – and all my shark fantasies came rushing in. He wanted to pull me into the middle of the pool; very gently, he did that. Then very slowly Rosie also angled up. They would sort of stay nearby so I could pat them, rub my hand over their skin, which was incredibly wonderful to feel.

I could feel something happening, and I very quickly realized that these beings were more inside of me than they were outside. I was not going to be able to relate to them through my conceptual mind – it was going to be irrelevant in that pool – so I flipped into intuitive, like going into overdrive. I let go, surrendered.

Within two minutes Rosie was straight up and down, pressed against my body; I was holding her and her fins were around me. I was in absolute ecstasy, kissing her on the mouth, saying, "Oh, Rosie! I love you so much! Oh, Rosie! Oh, God, Rosie!" No mind-model I had would have allowed me to do that; I just leaped out of it. Rosie was right there, and the way she was moving it was clear she was coming onto me – there was no doubt about it – and I started to get aroused. I started to think, is this legal?

I had been with an old colleague of mine, Tim Leary, a few weeks before, and Tim had said that he had gone swimming with the dolphins. I said, "Well, what was it like?" He said it was like making love. It was a very cold day, dark and gray. Everybody else was wearing a wetsuit, but I'd thought, gee, a wetsuit to make love is obscene. So I just went in my bathing trunks.

I held on to Rosie's fin. I didn't want to break the fin – it felt a little fragile, but it was really tough. We'd go down and dive, and swim around. Then I'd lose my grip. Finally I grabbed her around the belly and held onto the fin with my left hand. We went flying around under the water, on and on. Every time I'd think, she's a dolphin but I'm a human. I've got to come up for air, she would immediately come to the surface and wait for me to take a breath, and then go down again.

One time I came up and they were taking photographs and I got into my hammy-type thing of "me with the dolphins," you know? I was so busy with that that I forgot to get a breath. Rosie started to go down again, and I hadn't gotten the breath, and I thought, uh-oh. I'm gonna have to let go. I didn't get a breath! Immediately she came back up and waited for me to get a breath. I experienced that she had taken me into a place where she and I were hearing one another, we were tuned to one another.

After about 40 minutes I was shaking, I was so cold. You know, I'm fifty years old, and I'm cold, and I'm thinking I should get out, but I don't want to let go – this is ecstasy. At that moment, the minute I thought gee, I'm tired, she came right to the surface and violently pushed me away from her. She and Joe came around and put their noses against my stomach, and just pushed me right out of the pool. They wouldn't let me back into the pool. They would play with me from the edge of the pool, but they wouldn't let me come in. They played with my friend, who was wearing a wetsuit, but they wouldn't play with me anymore.

Here were John and his research crew trying to teach the dolphins the alphabet. I think that's great, it's admirable, I'm not knocking that research. But it just feels to me that the dolphins are great teachers. They were helping me get out of my rational mind and into my intuitive mind, and allowing us to be inside of each other. Because the far out thing is that when you go outside of the identification with body, and with personality, and with thought – you don't stop any of it, it's all going on, you take care of it – but when you go behind it, you come into a state of awareness that is no longer unique to you.

Shoveling Snow

It's a predicament when something inside of you happens that makes you go against all of the rules that previously were something you wouldn't have even considered going against. For example, after I took psilocybin the first time at Tim Leary's house, I went back to my parents' home in a big snowstorm. It was four in the morning, but I decided to shovel the snow. I felt healthy and alive, I was stoned out of my head, and there was all this snow. I felt like the young buck in the tribe. I'd shovel snow! I started to shovel the snow and my parents appeared at the upstairs window. They flung open the window – they assumed I was drunk — and said, "Come in, you goddamn idiot! Nobody shovels snow in the middle of the night!"

There was the voice of authority, and I had always listened to that. I was really a good boy, the whole trip. (That's how I got to be a Professor at Harvard, by always listening to what they said about when you shovel snow.) But inside my heart it was like, "You know, it's okay to shovel snow." Isn't that far out? Buoyed up by the drug, drugged out of my cultural/social/adaptive/other-directed mind, I was connected to an inner place that was saying, "Right on, baby. Shovel snow." Right at that moment all I did was look at my parents, smile, wave, and go back to shoveling snow.

And that was the beginning of a long melodrama in my life for the next few years, as I slowly saw myself going further and further away from the cultural rituals.

Eating Before Grace

There are ways of dealing with food as part of the process so that everything you do in life, and everything you have in life, becomes part of the awakening process. Like I have this delightful thing with my father. We sit at the table, and we're about to eat. He sits down, and as he sits down his hand is already on his fork, and even before the chair is pulled in the first bite of salad is in his mouth. He's crunching the lettuce, and he's halfway through the crunching of the lettuce when he realizes that I'm saying this blessing. He stops in mid-crunch, because he's gonna "wait until the kid finishes his blessing." But every now and then, if I take too long, I hear a crunch. He's pushing me a little bit, like, "Get on with it." It's a beautiful dialogue we go through. I don't try to lay it on too heavily; I just do it quietly to myself. I don't care if he eats his lettuce. I've told him that. "Oh, no, no. I won't eat my lettuce while you're praying."

He says to me, "What are you saying?" I tell him, but it doesn't do much for him. He joins in on the "Shanti, Shanti, Shanti" now, and then he says, "Amen." It's the best of all worlds.

Phyllis's Death

I watched my stepmother dying last year. She was a fine woman, but she had a tough ego; she was a tough lady. She had a lot of pain from cancer, and we did what we could to relieve the pain. We were very close and, as the time went on and the pain kept eating away and eating away and eating away, she kept saying, "I don't understand the pain." Her ego couldn't understand it, because she was losing control to the pain.

As the pain kept eating away and eating away, and as the time got closer towards death, she changed from being this tough ego and what appeared instead was this absolutely radiant being: peaceful, present, clear, loving, quiet. She died in my arms. There was no pushing, no pulling, no grabbing. There was no ego that I could see. It was just spirit going into spirit.

I thought, Oh, God! What a tough game this is. I never would have wished any of that on her, but I must admit that it broke through her defenses, and ego, and structure, and her addiction to Channel 2 in a way that nothing else could have done.

Now I've got to face the fact that my human heart loved her, and I would have taken away that suffering if I could. My higher wisdom sees the perfection of it – including my human heart and my desire to take away the suffering – and understands. That's the predicament you and I have to face. We have to embrace all of that – all of it – and then we can keep our hearts open. You can do what you do for another human being, but your equanimity stays perfectly clear. Unlike Job, you don't get lost in, "Why have you done this to me?" Because you understand. You may not intellectually understand, but you intuitively understand.

My attachment to my stepmother not suffering was wiping me out. It's really hard to keep that other plane going when you're dealing with family. "Ah, ha! Isn't everybody your family?" There's the one. I used to think, Oh, I'm so open. I love everybody the same. Until my step-mother got sick. Then I noticed, "Everybody's equal except my stepmother." Then my heart was really hurting, and when I didn't put the catheter in at the right time I had waves of guilt. I saw how corrosive that was – guilt is really corrosive.

I saw I had a long way to go until everybody's really my family. When it comes to physical suffering, it's a whole other ball game. That's the work we have to do. It's beautiful work.

The Telegram

Through all these years I have kept meditation going as another way of working on myself. During the summer of 1985, I spent two months in Rangoon, Burma, in a Theravadan meditation center. I worked with an extraordinary master named Sayadaw Upandita, sitting in meditation from three in the morning until 11 at night, following the rising and falling of the muscle in my abdomen that goes up and down with each breath.

It's one of the hardest things I ever did. I've done that meditation before, but I've never done it from three in the morning until 11 at night for two months. For ten minutes a day you see the teacher, and you report to the teacher. The report sounds like this: "6 p.m. last night I was meditating on the rising and falling of my breath. I was noting the rising as 'rising,' I was noting the falling as 'falling.' The rising had a quality of elasticity. The falling had a quality of settling. After about three minutes I became aware of the sound of a bird."

Then he interrupts and he says, "Did you hear the bird on a rising or a falling?"

You say, "I didn't notice."

He says, "Well, please try to be more attentive next time." As you're leaving he says, "By the way, did you go to sleep last night on a rising or a falling breath?" And it's extraordinary. It's a no-nonsense game, and he really sees where your mind is.

At the end of two months I got a telegram, which I'd been hoping and dreaming of getting the first month, but by the second month I had settled in and I was prepared to go the full three months that I had committed to do. Then at the end of the second month, unwanted now by me, a telegram came saying that my stepmother had cancer and was going to be operated on, and the prognosis was unclear. She was taking care of my father, and if she wasn't going to be around I should go back and take care of my father. That seemed obvious.

I took the telegram to the teacher, who had the telegram translated for him. He said, "Don't go."

"Don't go?"

He said, "You're really working to end suffering. You're doing very high work; you're very far along now, but you have more to do. If you leave now, you go back with the attachments you have, and what suffering will you relieve?" You may relieve a little short-term suffering, but in the long run you're just a "typhoid Mary," carrying suffering with you like everybody else. "Somebody else will take care of them; you stay here."

You know, in Hinduism when you become a sunyasin, a renunciate, they have a funeral ceremony for you; you die to your parents and family. But in the Jewish tradition . . . I mean, I'm a Jewish boy from Boston. You never die to your family. There was no shiva sat for me. He said, "I don't think you should go." And I looked, and I saw those samskaras, I saw my karma, the whole thing.

I said, "I hear what you're saying, but I've got to go." It's poignant, but there it is. And suddenly I went from "three in the morning to 11 at night in my meditation cell," to an intensive care ward, hours and days at a time. But it was extraordinary. So beautiful, and so clear, and so much love, and everybody was so liquid and human. It was just an incredible experience.

A Part to Play

When I was in Burma meditating, the first month I was just hoping a telegram would come that would allow me to escape. I wanted to be somebody who had gone to Burma to meditate, but I didn't really want to be there. By the second month I was cooling out, and then the telegram arrived, so I went home to be with her and to help out, taking care of Dad.

You listen to hear what part you play. I mean, what is free? Is there any form to freedom? Are you freer when you're in one form than another? No. What you end up doing is listening to hear what your unique part is to play. (Like a woman comes up to me and says, "I'd like to do spiritual work if it weren't for the children." Can you hear that? I mean the children are what's on her plate, so to speak. That's her vehicle through; it's not an error. The children are a vehicle to awaken; that's a method.)

The more I listen, the more I hear that I'm a member of a family, I'm a member of a community, I'm a member of a nation-state, I'm a member of an ecosystem, so I've got to vote, I've got to protest nuclear proliferation, I've got to be concerned about acid rain. I've got to do all this and, at the same moment, I've got to retain equanimity and do it all in some way that it keeps bringing me back into that spacious awareness so that I can offer that to everybody, to help everybody out of the entrapment of their drama.

So on my plate is taking care of my stepmother, and for some time there, it was taking care of my father. There was a period of several months when I was taking care of Dad. What was required was, you went in, you woke him up, got his legs over the side of the bed and helped him onto the walker, walked with him very slowly into the bathroom. Showering. Brushing teeth together. Toileting, wiping. Dressing. Walking on the walker into the kitchen. Preparing food. He eats. Pills. Insulin. To the chair.

I started to do this every morning. With somebody who is frail and old, sometimes the security of a structured routine makes them feel comfortable, so we do it the same way every day. Ah, but I'm not doing it the same way. After a while I notice that each day, in my mind I have a model of what I think I'm doing.

I started to keep a diary, and these are my entries. One day I'm busy being The Dutiful Son: "Hi, Dad. It's great to be here helping you out. I'm your son, Richard. Let's go." And I'm busy. I milk the drama for as much as I can, all the way through. It takes about two hours, and I'm just The Dutiful Son. Every move I make is such a dutiful son; I'm just perfect in my role.

The next day I notice in my diary that I was preoccupied with something, and I was Long Suffering all that morning: "C'mon, Dad, can't you walk a little faster?" There was no dutiful son then; I was busy being, "Oh, I've got to do this" and "Oh, well, all right. Come on, let's go."

The third day of this sequence, I was a Spiritual Teacher helping my father through transitions. "Dad, age is just . . ." You know, I'm doing that kind of routine.

Now you've got to understand my father. He's been living with "Rum Dum" for years, and he's just walking, sitting, shitting, bathing, dressing, walking, eating. He'll put up with all my crap. These are my mind trips, and he's just sitting, walking . . . He's right there all the time. I'm in my mind; he's not thinking anything, he's just doing it, see? While I've got these elaborate scenarios.

The next day I note in my diary that I'm concerned about what's going into Dad and what's coming out (because with older people you often have to equate those things). And I'm studying my father as a set of ambulatory variables. I'm The Scientist – "Well, Dad, we'll take a measure of this now."

Slow as I am, sooner or later even I saw that I was never with Dad – I was always in my mind. I was always thinking about what I was doing, I was always creating these incredible mythic scenarios of what I was doing. I was always rehearsing, and planning, and remembering, and all that, and I was never there. It took quite a while to quiet down enough.

It's interesting: I go to Rangoon, Burma, on the other side of the earth to practice meditation. The moving meditation is walking: lift your leg, push it forward, place it down; lift, push, place; lift, push, place. You keep your awareness with it. I go all the way around the world to do that, and it takes me two months to realize that as I'm walking behind my father in the walker, he's doing "lift, push, place; lift, push, place," while I'm busy saying, "Come on, Dad, let's go!"

See, my model in Rangoon is, "I'm meditating!" My model here is, "I'm taking care of Dad." The minute the models go, there is scrubbing, dressing, walking, driving, sleeping, loving, eating, looking, smelling . . . just the present moment, the richness of it all. Suddenly Dad and I are together, like Rosie and I were together, like Juan and I were together, like Maharajji and I were together. We're in the space together and all the models are gone, and I'm no longer a thought away from where Dad is, and the energy is incredible, and I am in ecstasy. I'm so happy. I feel foolish, I'm so happy doing it.

My brother, who's a lawyer, says to me, "Rich, it's really great the way you're taking care of Dad." Which sort of means he doesn't want to do it. (I don't want to badmouth my brother 'cause he's a caring person. He just didn't want to do that particularly.) I milk it for what I can. I say to him, "Well, Bill, somebody's gotta do it." You think I'm going to tell him that it's the highest thing I do all day, and that I'd pay to do it?

Now I give that just as an example of taking something in life that is on your plate. When you listen, you hear who you are and what your unique function is in the universe. And you hear which kind of suffering is yours to take on. Some people, it is perfect that they work with the homeless. Some people, it is perfect that they work for people in Third World countries. Some people, it is perfect that they raise their children with love and presence and caring and compassion. Each person has a unique way through. Each person has a part to play.

Krishna in Drag

I'm driving my old Buick and a State Trooper stops me for going so slow. (I seem to have a lot of karma with police. Not like some of my friends, but . . .) The State Trooper stops me, and I'm going too slow because I'm driving an antique car, and he says, "You're going too slow."

I say, "Yes, Officer." I'm the potential criminal, and he's the policeman. I've been doing mantra for some hours and I'm so out of my skull that I look at him and he is obviously Krishna, who is in drag. He's appearing to be a State Trooper who's come to give me a ticket, but he's really come to let me see God in this form. But I know you don't say to him, "Hey, I know you're not a State Trooper, you're God," because therein lies much trouble, you know?

So we play out our routines. Then we run out of the routine of culprit and policeman. But he's feeling good, because every time I look at him I'm totally in love with him. I mean I don't want to go to bed with him, I'm just in love with him. "Are you here? I'm here. Far out. Here we are. Well, if you want to be the policeman, I'll be the culprit. Okay. Here we go."

You and I have to dance in form. There's no way we can meet on this plane other than through our forms. The only question is whether we get lost in the melodrama.

So the State Trooper doesn't want to leave because it feels so good. Of course, it feels so good to resonate free of our separateness for a moment. He says, "Great car you got here." because that's another kind of macho thing men can talk about. We kick the tires, and spit, and do all the things you're supposed to do. Then we sort of run through that routine, and he says, "Well, be gone with you." Great.

I start to drive away, and he's gone back to his police car. I look in the rearview mirror and he's waving at me. I'm about to stop and say, "You blew it now. Because State Troopers don't wave. C'mon, I mean, you're not playing your game cleanly enough."

Indian Railway Station

I was raised as a middle-class, well toilet-trained American, and I found myself some years ago in India in a train station. The train was going to be two days late, which is not unusual in India, and I was low on funds so I was going to have to stay there at the station. I had a bad case of dysentery, which meant I had to go to the toilet every twenty minutes or so. The latrine had gotten plugged up about a year earlier, so you had to sort of step between the piles of feces to find a place to squat – and I was barefoot, because I was being a sadhu. And flies – there were millions of flies everywhere.

Railway stations are very extraordinary in India. All of life lives there. There were hundreds of people living in the station, waiting for trains; there were chickens and goats and babies, and everybody was screaming and peeing and vomiting all over the floor. It was teeming with life. I was drinking watery tea out of a cracked cup that was dripping all over my dhoti. You sit on the cement floor . . . and you sit there. You're going to sit for two days.

Everything in my training said, "This is hell!" I mean, my mother told me this would happen if I wasn't good! But there was a part of me that was happy. It was enough – it just was what was. Okay, here we are. Ah, so. I couldn't believe it. My mind wouldn't let me believe that I was content at that moment. It kept saying, "You must be insane to be happy under these conditions. You have no right to be happy here!"

It's extraordinary to start to rest in the place in your being where whatever it is, it's enough.

Side B:
The Rarities

Side B: The Rarities

When You Go Out, Look at the Stars

A tree is a tree, and a river is a river, and you're you. That's why when somebody loses connection with things, put them as close to nature as you can. Give them a rock, or light a candle, or take them out and show them the stars.

I remember once I was on an acid trip with a number of the pushers in San Francisco. It was a very essence, invitation-only trip. There was incredible music, and colors on the ceiling, all very beautiful. This was very very pure LSD and I'd taken quite a bit of it. I went up very fast, like an elevator, because it's a way of overriding the realities you thought were real. I got to this space, and I was going out when I felt something in my field that wasn't comfortable.

I looked over, and there was a young fellow having a very bad time. The chemical was strong and pushing and he couldn't release. He was frightened and got paranoid; he got tighter and tighter. There was my host, who was trying to solve the problem without disturbing me. He was reading from *The Psychedelic Experience*, which is a book that I was a co-author of. I could hear that he was not reading it with great faith.

I felt myself pulled back into my separateness. I went over and I fell down on top of this kid and I said, "All right. You've got all of our consciousnesses. What do you want to do with them?" He was so panicked, he turned to me and said, "I'm going to take my girlfriend, and I'm going to get on my motorcycle, and I'm going to go home. I'm going to get my .38 and I'm going to come back and blow your fucking brains out!" He said it with all the hate and loathing of a full paranoid episode.

I said to him, "Well, if you do that you're going to kill a really beautiful guy. But if you're gonna do it, you're gonna do it. We're all your friends. We'll be here. You go do what you've gotta do." He got up and pulled his girlfriend after him. He went to the door, and just as he was about to leave I said, "By the way, when you go out, you may not trust any of us, because we're humans and we're not very trustworthy. But look up at the stars, because they've been around. They won't con you."

He went out and closed the door. We all were sort of stunned by what had happened. Maybe two or three minutes later the door burst open and he fell into the room, sobbing. And he was through.

Now I know that some of you are scared to death by methods as violent as that, and I can understand that fear. I think we must be very careful about them. But I wanted to share with you the way in which your connection to that which is intuitively, harmoniously connected is a healing factor. Like in old folks' homes. When they allow the old folks to have even a plant (let alone a puppy dog!), they are healthier and happier because of that connection to nature.

Assets and Liabilities

All the guys I hung out with in the Himalayas have been on another trip. While we've been busy going to the moon, they've been developing yoga. While we've been concerned with what we can find out and control of the universe through our senses and through our rational minds, they've been saying, "Well, that's all very interesting, but that's the problem. That's the limit. That's the illusion." They see the senses and the mind are the illusion, while we in the West say, "Those are our assets." One group of people says it's our assets, the other group says it's our liability.

I lived with a family in India who has a little daughter who is deaf and mute. Now in the West when you live in a family where there is a deaf-mute, everybody is completely obsessed with pity, with super-kindness. This family is a very, very pure family, they're very high, and they live in another universe than we do. As far as they're concerned, this is the privileged child in the scene. This child didn't happen to be hung up with those senses, and therefore is like an angel.

The whole place is sort of designed around the worship of this child. Not in any grotesque fashion – they don't keep her in golden robes sitting on throne. But she came in when I was sleeping to wake me. She had been watching the sunrise, and she came in to describe the sun rising to me: "Ahhh, ooohh, ooooo." She put me on such a trip. She was so high, so stoned out of her head.

We've got to go a long way to change the model in our heads about who that child is. "Poor kid. I mean, that's all very nice, but poor kid. She can't do all the things that other kids can do."

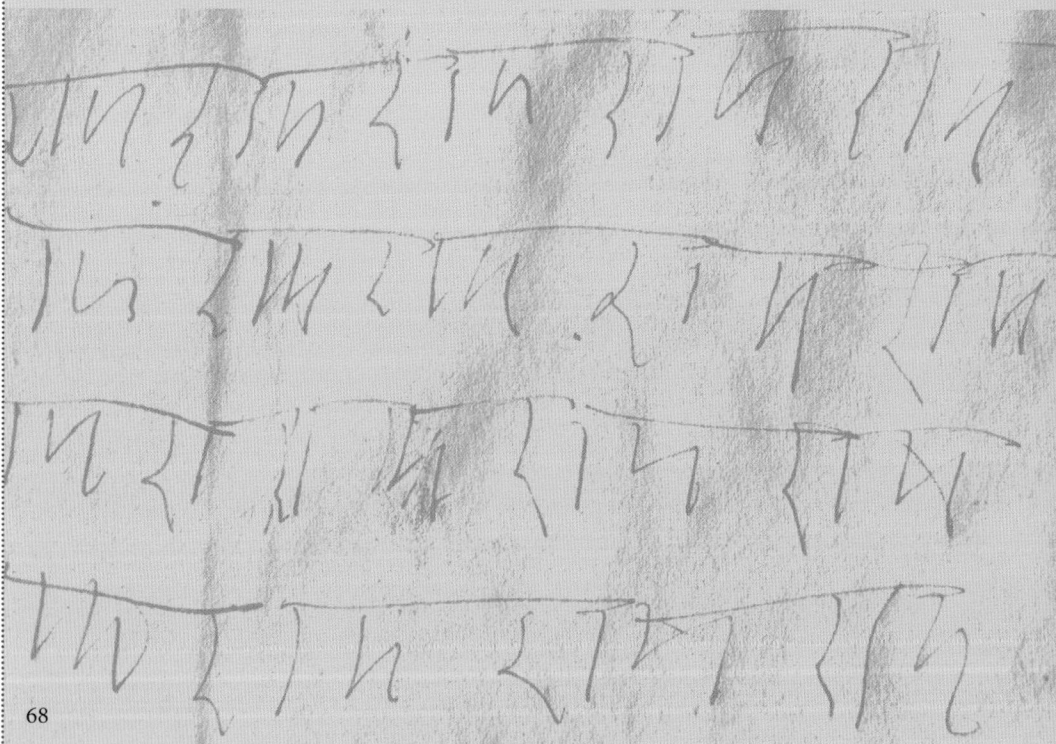

The Creamed Vegetable Circuit

One day I was sitting with a group of people with my guru, and there was a Supreme Court judge there. My guru usually ignored me; he'd make a big thing out of me for a moment or two, but he ignored my past all the time and I never knew he knew anything about it.

This particular time he introduced me to the judge and he said, "This is a very important professor from America." (Of course it wasn't true, but my guru lied like a rug – that's the first thing we must notice about realized beings.) He built me up incredibly as someone very important, very significant in America, and he showed the judge!

The judge said, "Well, perhaps Ram Dass would like to visit the Supreme Court."

Now I come from a family of lawyers, and I came to India to find living spirit and God and I really didn't anticipate finding it in the Supreme Court, so I really didn't want to do it. But when he said, "perhaps Ram Dass would like to," and he looked at me, I did that thing you do under those conditions and I said, "Oh, that would be very nice."

So he said, "Tomorrow?"

I realized I was getting trapped. I said, "Well, you'll have to ask my guru," figuring he'd get me off the hook.

Maharajji said to him, "If he said it will be very nice, it'll be very nice. Tomorrow." See? And then he pointed at me, like: "Don't lie if you don't want to get caught!"

I went to the court, and I went through the murder trials, and I did my whole business. I was being taken around by this very important judge. When we came into the room where all of the young lawyers were in their black robes, they saw, even though I was dressed as a sadhu (as a kind of Western hippie), that I was still a Westerner, and I was with the judge, so they all surrounded me. At that time, Nixon had been making overtures to China, which was concerning India a great deal. They asked me about Nixon's China policy. I had read Time magazine, so I was proficient to speak about anything. I gave a very profound answer (as profound as you can get in Time).

Then I went back to Maharajji and he asked, "What happened?" When I'd start to tell him, he'd tell me things that had happened (which is what he always did to play with my mind). So he kept playing with me and finally he sent me away.

That evening at the gathering there was a lawyer. He looked just like a lawyer. He said to me, "I was in the Bar Association room today, and I'd like to invite you to speak to the Rotary Club and to speak to the Bar Association."

I thought, Oh my God, this is going to be terrible! I'm going to end up in India on the 'creamed vegetable circuit.' This is not what I had in mind when I came to India. Now I had learned my lesson from the last time, so I was going to be all truth now. I said, "Well, I don't want to do any of it. But if my guru says I must, I will."

So he went up to my guru and he said, "Maharajji, we'd like Ram Dass to speak to the Bar Association and the Rotary Club."

Maharajji said, "Really? Wonderful!" And he turned to all the Indian devotees and said, "Isn't this magnificent? Ram Dass is going to speak . . ."

I thought, That rat is selling me down the river. This is a terrible thing. Here I went truth this time, and he's undercutting me.

The lawyer was all smiles, and then Maharajji said to me, "What are you going to speak about?" I had no idea what I was going to speak about. I'd never planned to speak. But I thought, Well, dharma is law and these lawyers are lawyers, so I said, "I'm going to speak about the dharma and the law."

"Accha!" – that's good. He said, "Are you going to speak about Christ?"

I said, "Of course!" (Because you get the clue about how to be a good guy.)

He says, "Accha. Are you going to speak about Hanuman?"

I said, "Oh, of course I'm going to speak about Hanuman!"

He said, "Are you going to speak about me?"

I said, "Of course! You're my guru. How could I not speak about you?"

"Accha!"

The lawyer said, "Well, actually Maharajji, we thought that Ram Dass would speak about Nixon's China policy."

Maharajji looked absolutely shocked! He said, "Nixon's China policy! You could never trust Ram Dass to speak about a thing like that! Ram Dass only talks about God."

I said, "Yes. That's right! All I can talk about is God."

The lawyer said, "Well, in that case, maybe I'll just have a few lawyers over to my house. I don't think it would be right for the Rotary club and the Bar Association."

I got my clue, and it's been helpful again and again and again. Because almost every night before I lecture I sit alone in the dark and I say to God, "Well, what am I doing here? What's this all about? What is it I'm supposed to do?"

I remember this story, and I realize all I have to do is speak about God.

Death at Rainbow Gathering

A few years ago I was at the Rainbow Gathering in Roseburg, Oregon, living with the Hog Farm. I was in the tent, and in the middle of a very hot day a couple walked up and came in. They asked if would I marry them. Why not? The Hog Farm got a watermelon and cut it like a wedding cake. We had a ceremony, and they kissed and went off happily.

Just after they'd gone, somebody rushed up and said, "Is there a doctor here?" There happened to be two doctors and they went rushing up, because somebody had fallen off the mountain. It turned out to be a young fellow, maybe 19 years old. I went along.

He was lying naked, kind of broken up and cracked, among a set of rocks. Gash in his forehead, bubbly breathing. The doctors started to do their doctor thing, like move him to a flat place, careful of these bones, breathe, and explaining to him what he should do to stay alive. Now I'm in the dying business, you see, and it looks like my services may be called into play here, but I can't push the doctors: "Excuse me, I've got to prepare this person to die."

I knew that when there is a violent or traumatic accident, a person is usually pushed out of their bodies. He's just floating around anyway, so I'll just talk to him. I sat down on a rock and started to talk to him. I said, "You probably didn't expect this, but the first thing you should know," which the Bardo Thodol instructs you to say, "You should know that you may be about to be dead. And you probably have a choice. Your body is kind of cracked up, but we could probably put it back together again. You can see better than I, and you ought to make a choice."

Well, at any rate, soon his bubbling stopped and the body died. It was getting late in the day. I knew it would be nice to keep the body there for three days, but politically that wasn't going to be possible, obviously. Helicopters were on their way. So they took the body in a blanket down the mountain, and I decided that I would sit up on the mountain for a while and talk to this being. I would explain everything I understood about what he might be going through, and any help that I could give him, because I know that beings that have just died are clairvoyant. They can pick up anybody's mind, and they're very tuned to minds where there is a love connection. What makes it difficult is that most of those love connections are pulling on the person and there's a lot of confusion. They're saying, "Come back!" but the body is no longer habitable by the consciousness, and they're very confused by those messages. Sometimes they look into people's minds, and they're full of, "Thank God he's dead! Let's find his will!" And they get so angry that they want vengeance. Those are the angry ghosts that are always haunting places and scaring people.

So I sat down and I talked to this guy. I talk to people when they die, and usually I have a sense of the presence of the being. (That can be just my psychosis. Who knows? But my experience is that there is a presence of these beings.) But this time I didn't feel a thing. It's like, "Are you there? Hello? Hello?" And, "Here's how it is, are you hearing me? Well, I'll send it anyway, maybe your transmitter isn't tuned right or something."

I stayed for about an hour, but I was very perplexed. Because here was this young kid who's fallen off a mountain, probably high on something, naked, and he's bashed up, and he should be hanging around here confused. Where is he? I figure, well, this is just something in my head. Probably I wasn't pure enough at this moment to pick him up.

A few hours later somebody came along and said, look, this is the fellow who saw him last, and he'd like to tell you the story of what he saw.

The fellow said, "I was standing down below, and I saw him come to the front of the mountain. He was naked, and he put his arms out, and he walked off the mountain. He fell halfway down against some rocks. I rushed up to him, and saw he was badly cut. I helped him to sit down, and I said, 'You wait here, don't move. I'll go get help.' I went running away. I looked back and he had stood up, and he was saying, 'Christ! Christ! I'm coming!'" And he walked off the rest of the mountain."

Now, I mean . . . He's a 19-year-old kid, dying at a Rainbow Gathering. It's hardly the way to go. Poor kid. He could have lived 50 more years. See? Who was that? What was that one about?

The way one dies is not random; it's connected with one's karma.

Microphone as Guru

The other night I came in to give a lecture. I like a certain kind of microphone with a mini-boom because it allows me to come up close and still sit cross-legged. I don't like the straight microphones, because I've got to lean forward all evening. So I specify to the people who are arranging a lecture that I want it a certain way.

I came into the hall all full of love and sweetness. Oh, here's Ram Dass. Oh, he's so beautiful. Oh, hello everybody. Oh, yes. I'm so holy, and I smell of roses. Then I walk in and I see this straight microphone, and I say, "What's that doing here!"

The woman who's the manager says, "Well, that's the only microphone we have."

I said, "Well, didn't I order a different one? This isn't acceptable at all!"

I saw myself turn into this vicious, cold, manipulative person . . . and then I broke out laughing. I realized that my guru had come in drag as a microphone, see?

Got you again, you phony holy!

Nepali Baba

I was with a yogi astrologer named Nepali Baba outside of Bombay a few years ago. He was a beautiful guy, a very simple man. I came with a friend, in a taxi, unannounced. There were some women in the room – a very simple cement room – each with her birth chart, waiting to get his astrological interpretation.

I'd heard a lot of stories about him. A woman, a friend of a friend, came to him because her husband had died and for two weeks there was this rattling all over the house. He said, "Well, the problem is that your husband is trying to tell you he buried the box with all the securities and the money, and he didn't tell you where it was. I'll show you." And he went to the place and dug it up. There were a lot of stories about him like that.

So I went to him, and he did pretty good. He said, "You had an Indian guru." I said yes. "He died."

"Yes.

"You're going to have his darshan again when you're 56 and when you're 63."

I thought, That's great! Wow. I'll wait around for that. "Am I going to be at all conscious when I die?"

"Oh, you're going to choose the moment of your death. You're going to die when you're about 82 or 83."

Ever since then I don't worry about anything.

Chicken Karma

When I was in India I had been vegetarian for a long time. One time we stayed at this hotel, the Palace Heights, which was the hippie hangout in Connaught Circus.

It turned out that the window in the room we had overlooked the alley next to a fancy restaurant. The Indians are going Western these days in Delhi, and at that restaurant they served chicken. They'd wring the necks of the chickens out in the alley.

Every afternoon around 4 o'clock, we'd come back from shopping, and suddenly we'd hear, "Cluck, cluck, cluck" . . . krraaaccch. And I felt all my chicken karma, all the Sunday chicken dinners I was paying for. There was another one, and another . . .

It's interesting. Recently I've gone to Col. Sanders. Knowing the horror of it all, not only the physical horror of the way the chickens are produced, but also the absurdity of asking them to produce a chicken so I can eat it. But I eat it and enjoy it. And I sit with that horror. Because I can't be phony holy anymore. I've just got to be where I'm at.

Eating for Pleasure

In a series of ashramic situations, I've been responsible for having a huge feast cooked. We all plan that this is going to be the final feast. Everybody gets excited preparing the feast. The table is laid out, the food's placed on the table, everybody's anticipating, been building up their hunger and desire.

Then I usually start with a long blessing of the food, and you can see that the cooks are thinking, The food's getting cold! I ask that we keep doing the blessing until everybody is doing the blessing, so the cooks have to give up thinking about the food getting cold in order to do the blessing. When the blessing's finished, I say, "Before we eat, I'd like to read to you the Buddhist meditation on the repulsiveness of food," which I then do. At that point the cooks don't really care whether the food is cold or not. Then I start in saying, "The way we will eat," and proceed to give a mindful-eating practice of lifting, lifting, putting, putting, tasting, tasting.

By then the banquet is ruined. Think of all the years you've been eating for your own pleasure. How much does it cost to surrender a little of that pleasure in order to become mindful of the process of eating?

Those of you who have a weight problem will notice that, if you focus on getting thin, you'll be suffering all the time, but if you become mindful of eating, you will get thin. And those of you who are into cooking and into the exquisite subtleties of food, there's nothing wrong with any of that – that can be done as a yoga, too.

But we have gone so far overboard in sense gratification that our ability to comprehend the use of food as merely survival and maintaining the body has almost been lost completely. Especially because we don't demand-feed, we schedule-feed at 8, 12, and 6, or whatever.

Part of what sadhana is about is experimentation with each of the aspects of your life, and one of those aspects is eating.

The Sattvic Trap

Let me work with the issue of diet a little more. I stopped eating meat, fish, chicken and eggs some years back. For seven years I was a vegetarian. I got slightly superior about it. I was a vegetarian back before it was popular. Way back in '64 I was being quoted on macrobiotics, saying it gets you high.

Then I got into the predicament where I thought, You know, I think maybe I've gotten caught in what's called the sattvic trap. I'm caught in being a good guy and I ought to sort of undercut it. So what I'd better do is break my vegetarian trip just to break it. And since I was raised as a Jew, I might as well really do the trip up and have spare ribs, which would hit it from both angles.

I found a Chinese restaurant; it was one of those dark ones. I went there one afternoon while I was on the road to New Hampshire. I went in and ordered the spareribs. I blessed them – I gave a particularly long blessing. I offered them to Maharajji. I said to him, "I know you think this is strange, but it's the way it is. You know my heart, and you know why I'm doing it, and I'm just going to do it." Then I proceeded to thoroughly enjoy the spareribs. They were as good as I remembered them being.

There was a man sitting about two booths away – suit and tie, and a gold wristwatch. He was drinking tea through my whole meal; drinking tea and watching me. Finally he came over and said, "May I sit down for a minute?"

Sure.

He said, "I'm a traveling salesman for an electronics outfit at M.I.T., and I couldn't help watching the way you blessed the food. The blessing was so powerful, I haven't been able to leave the restaurant!" It turned out that he was a fundamentalist Christian, and we got into a beautiful rap about the Bible and Christ. We talked for about an hour and a half, and drank a lot of tea.

Finally he said, "I'm so delighted to have met you. It's wonderful. You know, I've had a lot of trouble with my diet. What do you eat?"

I looked down, and right in front of me was this pile of bones. I would have done anything to be able to push it away and say, "Well, I'm a vegetarian." But all I could say was, "You're looking at it."

Two Potatoes

This story concerns the issue of whether you and I are in law or outside of law, and how we deal with issues of righteousness. It concerns a sadhu named Sombari Maharaj, up in the Himalayas. One day he came out of his cave and said to one of his devotees, "Here are two potatoes. Take them down to the river and eat both potatoes." That's like an order from the guru.

So the devotee went down to the river and he started to eat the potatoes. He was halfway through the first potato when a beggar appeared and said, "Babaji, Babaji, you have two potatoes, I have none! Give me one of your potatoes."

The devotee thought, I have two potatoes, how can I keep the other potato? Righteousness? There it is. So he gave the beggar the second potato.

Later the devotee came back to Sombari Maharaj, who had been in his cave some distance away, out of sight of the river. Sombari Maharaj came out screaming at him: "You fool! You idiot! You gave away the second potato! Ah, well, that's your bhagya – your destiny."

The person who told me that story said, "That devotee went on to be a judge. He had five children, who all made good marriages. He was a very highly respected citizen. He lived a very happy and successful life. Of course, that was the first potato."

Turned out the beggar was Sombari Maharaj, just testing the devotee.

Can you hear that story? Can you hear going behind righteousness out of compassion? That's an interesting one.

Two Boats

There's this boatman rowing along on the river one morning. The fog is thick and suddenly he bumps another boat. He starts to scream profanities at the other boatman for not looking where he was going. The fog clears for a moment; he looks at the other boat and sees that it's empty.

That's really the essence of the situation with relationships. All those things we're getting angry at, all those things we're fascinated by in the other person, they are all just things happening, and we keep identifying them with people.

Best Teachings

At one point when I was in India, I had a sexual relationship with a fellow who was another devotee. When we came before Maharajji, I was freaked to think that Maharajji knew that I had done this. He looked at this guy and said to me, "Ah, you've given him your best teachings."

That has hung with me over these years; you can imagine what effect that had! I mean, was he saying . . . Oh, no, he couldn't be saying that! What was he saying?

I have to live with that unknown all the time as to all the stuff about sexuality. All I can hear is that I'm not going to end up a horny celibate. I know I can't play with people sexually — "Come on up and see my holy pictures" — because I want something.

All I know is I hear the idea that I have to be truthful with people. If I let lust intervene between me and the person, I lose another connection to my heart and I can't afford that.

Lepers at the Ghats

I was in Banaras, and I went to the bathing ghats. We came to a whole, long line of lepers—there were maybe 125 of them, and they all had begging bowls. They were all in different degrees of decay.

We divided up our coins, and I had about 20 coins. I started to walk down this line, and started to hold up the coin, and saw all the hands reaching out. I found myself trying to decide whether not having a nose was worse than not having two feet. Then I thought, How bizarre! Was a woman with half of her face eaten away worse or better than somebody who was on a wooden skid, pushing himself along with his elbows?

I had to open. It pushed me outside of my discriminative mind into my intuitive mind. I went along handing out coins until they was gone. All the time I was looking into everybody's eyes – looking into the eyes of the person I handed it to, and the people I didn't. What was extraordinary was that most of them were right here. The guilt would have been mine, not theirs; they weren't laying it on me – I was buying it out of my own mind. The minute I was free of it, I could do what I had to do, they were doing what they had to do, and here we are. Your trip through leprosy? You should hear my problems! Heavy duty – and here we are.

I don't know how you can respond to the infinite, subtle varieties of suffering that exist in the universe other than intuitively. You cannot do it rationally, or it's going to drive you up the wall.

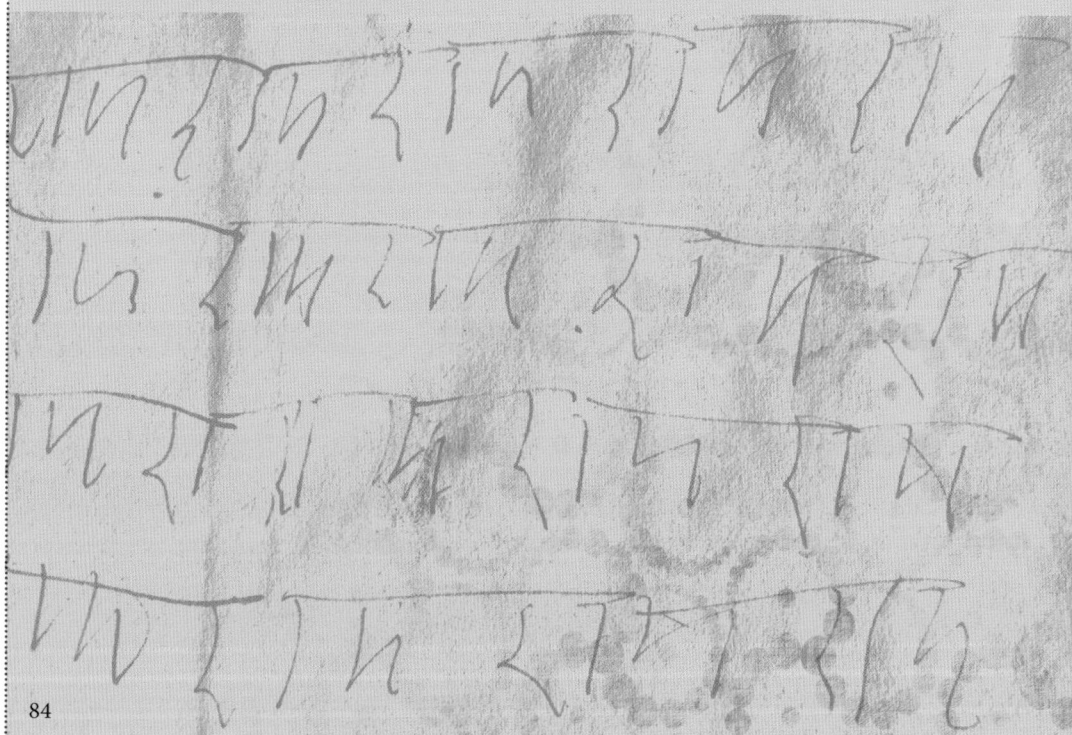

Identify Yourself

There's a great Nasrudin story. Nasrudin is that Sufi rascal, a spiritual madman. He went into a bank to cash a check, a very large check, but he's very disreputable looking. He handed the check to the teller, and the teller studied the check, looked it over very carefully. The check looked fine, but Nasrudin was somewhat suspect. So the teller said to Nasrudin, "Well, the check looks all right, but can you identify yourself?"

Nasrudin reached into his pocket, pulled out a mirror, looked into it and said, "Yep, that's me!" See, he was up-leveling the game.

Ravana

In the Ramayana, which is the story of Ram and Hanuman, Ram is God and Ram's wife is stolen away by Ravana, who is the bad guy. Ravana is a demon; he has ten heads, and twenty arms, and he's extremely powerful. He has all the gods scared, everybody scared. Very, very heavy-duty ego, like Nixon.

But it turns out that Ravana happens also to be a very high yogi, who is cleaning up his act by taking birth to do that. It's like Central Casting saying, "Who wants to play the heavy? Who's gonna play Lady Macbeth?"

"Okay, I'll play Lady Macbeth."

You begin to focus on what is behind someone's manifestations of good and evil, so you don't close your heart. You see God peeking out through all this stuff, even though you may be in the role where you're gonna say, "No, you may not," or "Yes, you may," or "I'm going to stop you from doing what you're doing."

The Man Who Sang Kaddish

I was giving a darshan in the Universalist Church in Central Park West in New York City some years back, and there was an Indian musician by the name of Pranath who was joining me. The church is set up so that on the back wall there is a huge mural of Christ washing the feet of one of his disciples. I was there, all in white, with flowers. (That was the time, as I recall, when my father was sitting in the back with his new wife-to-be, and at one point he leaned over and said, "You know, I feel just like the Virgin Mary.")

As Pranath was singing, a man came up, dressed completely in black leather, and he had a black cross. After Pranath stopped, this man walked to the center of the church and kneeled down facing the mural and sang Kaddish – the prayer for the dead in Hebrew. It was an extraordinarily powerful moment, because he was really a good cantor. I felt it was a great addition to the moment.

He finished and moved off to the side, and I did my thing. Then we were all done and we started singing "Hare Krishna." The audience was all up and into it, and I got dancing (which I sometimes do). I stood up, and I had my eyes closed and my arms out and I was dancing, and I suddenly felt these two wet things on the palms of my hands. Somebody had given me a box of strawberries earlier and this fellow had taken two strawberries and ground them into my hands, like the stigmata. I was aware at that moment that somebody had loaned us an Oriental rug, and that I shouldn't let the strawberries drop on the Oriental rug. You've got to remember your zip code, you've got to keep it all together at every level. So I grabbed the strawberries and sat down on the stage and ate them.

At that point, the man stood up and started to exhort everybody about Armageddon, and the impurity of their actions, and how they were going to be cast into hell. The audience listened for about four of five minutes, and then they started to "Om." He kept on doing this in a very loud voice, and the Om-ing kept getting louder until it was like ocean waves of Om. His voice would come out, and then it would disappear into the waves of Om, and then it would come out again. I went over and sat next to him, and we started to hold hands. It turned into a more and more beautiful art form of the spirit because everybody realized the purity of his statement, whether or not we agreed with it.

Afterwards he and I went out and meditated in Central Park together. It was a very beautiful moment.

A Kitten in Goa

I was in Goa with a friend. We were on the beach, doing the things that you do on beaches in Goa, sort of that other form of spirituality. We were going to get the last bus to go into the town to go out to dinner, because we didn't have any food where we were staying.

Just as we were about 150 yards from the bus stop, I looked over to the side and saw a tiny kitten. Its arms and legs were splayed out, its fur standing up on its back, and it was clearly in a state of terror. In that second, I saw the whole situation about life and death, all of it, right there, fully clear.

Knowing full well what would then follow, I said to my friend, "Look at that." He looked, and hearts opened. We calmed the kitten down, and then we looked to see whose home the cat came from. Everybody in the neighborhood said they didn't want a cat. Then somebody said that somebody had left three kittens – thrown them down into the gully – and two of them had died. This was the only one that was left, and they were waiting for it to die. Because they were living close to subsistence, and they had lots of cats and lots of dogs and lots of cows, they knew that was the way things were.

Well, we looked to see whether there was a nursing mother, because I figured maybe I could buy the services of the nursing mother cat. No, nothing. So we ended up with the kitten back at the room, with a medicine dropper and baby formula, feeding this baby kitten. Well, day after day, it was clearly very sick and frightened. It quieted down but it was still terribly sick. We took a closet and put our shirts down in it (which the cat was shitting all over), and we kept feeding it. It was crying in the middle of the night so we had to take turns getting up every few hours. Then we were going to leave Goa, but we couldn't leave with the kitten, and we couldn't leave the kitten, so we had to change our plans. Two weeks later – we were waiting for the cat to be strong enough to travel – the kitten died. We had a nice burial.

You know, as you're walking along and you see something like that, do you say, "Leaves fall. Death is catching the bus." Or do you stop, even though you know? Do you stay open to those feelings and those situations, or do you close your heart down?

The Pot That Died

My best story about not getting caught in expectations concerns Nasrudin, the mad mystic. One day he goes to his neighbor and says, "Can I borrow your big pot?"

The neighbor says, "Nasrudin, you are extremely irresponsible. It would be really unwise of me to give you this big pot."

Nasrudin says, "By everything that's sacred, I promise I will return the big pot. I will return it! I'll return it tomorrow."

Finally, against his better judgment, the neighbor loans the pot.

The next morning, bright and early, there is Nasrudin knocking on the door with the pot. The neighbor says, "Nasrudin! You've returned the pot!" The neighbor looks down at the pot and sees that there's a little, teeny pot inside it. The neighbor says, "What's that?"

Nasrudin says, "The big pot had a baby."

So the neighbor said, "Oh, thank you very much." And he closed the door.

About two weeks later Nasrudin appeared at the door and he said, "Could I borrow your big pot?"

The neighbor said, "Of course you can!" So Nasrudin takes the pot. Next day, no pot. Day after, no pot. The neighbor can't stand it; he goes to Nasrudin and says, "Nasrudin! Where's my pot?" Nasrudin said, "It died."

Heathrow

A few years back I was attending the World Humanities Conference, which had Members of Parliament, and Ruth Carter Stapleton, and all kinds of impressive people. I was on the program, and I was to be met by dignitaries.

Except that I didn't get through customs.

I wasn't carrying anything, but I was on a list that said that I was "not conducive to the well-being of the United Kingdom," mainly because of my affiliation with Timothy Leary. So I was detained, and then I was thrown out of the country.

Now, I had planned to arrive and be welcomed and taken to a hotel, and instead I found myself sitting in this green room with guys guarding the doors. I was sitting there with Pakistanis, and South Africans, and all these people who were also not conducive to the well-being of the United Kingdom. We were a great group and we had a wonderful day. It took me a few minutes to go from "What?" to "Wow! This is a much more interesting day than I expected to spend."

It's always a question of how long it takes you to let go.

The Carpenter

The winter I was writing *How Can I Help?* I was housesitting a beautiful farm for some friends. The first Sunday I was there, the people who owned the house had not yet gone to India, and we were all hanging out together. I was getting ready to settle in to work that week.

A fellow came by who was going to do some carpentry around the house. He came in to see me, introduced himself and said, "I wanted you to know that I'm very happy I'm going to be doing the carpentry here, because I've read your books, and I want to tell you it's meant a lot to me." He was a very beautiful guy, and he was clearly not only saying that; he was also saying, "I hope we can hang out together this week."

I started to get that feeling, "Here I come to this farm to be alone and now, the first day, this guy's gonna be doing carpentry every day . . ." So I emitted some kind of vibration that said, "Oh, that's lovely." I was happy to meet him, but I didn't want to . . . You hear?

Then the fellow whose house it was explained to this young fellow that during the week I needed to be alone to work and that he should come do the carpentry on weekends. He understood perfectly, and didn't want to bother me, and drove away. It was all very gentle and very understanding.

On Wednesday he put a shotgun in his mouth and blew his head off.

So what's a book about helping worth? Was I so busy with my model of where I thought I was going to do good that I couldn't be open to that moment? Now, you can mea culpa yourself, or you can just . . . yeah . . . part of the human condition.

Reincarnation

I was a psychologist in one recent incarnation, and a student of personality research. I would study parents and children and try to predict why children were the way they were in view of how the parents had been, and in view of their environment; heredity and environment as we in psychology measured it.

We had high-powered computers, and we would measure everything that was measurable in the parents, and everything that was measurable in the environment that we, in our sophisticated and theoretical way, would understand to be determinants of how you'd come out being who you are. We would feed it all into a computer and out would come a prediction of who you were. Then we would measure who you are, and we would see how close our prediction was to who, in fact, you came out to be. It was building a body of knowledge about cause and effect, assuming that you were totally the product of this life's environment and heredity.

The best correlations we ever got in that kind of research – and we were average for the course – was roughly about 0.5. A 0.5 correlation means that you are explaining about 25% of the variability. That means if I pick you and try to predict who you are because I know everything about you in this lifetime, about 25% of your whole picture is all I could possibly predict; the other 75% just comes out strange. About which I then as a social scientist say, "Well, that's due to error of measurement. Or it's due to the fact that we just aren't complex enough in our system."

It never enters my mind as a psychologist that my theory might be wrong, because you get very wedded to your theories, especially when you've come out of a behavioral tradition of philosophical materialism. But that 75% of the variability leaves ample space for reincarnation theory. And we are continually faced, in terms of anecdotes, with people, who, like Mozart create sonatas at four, give public recitals at five, and compose their first opera at seven.

Or a little girl in India, who at seven years old, tells her father, "Look, I was living in another village and I've got two children and I must go visit them right away!" She persuades him to take her there. She tells her father all about how the village has changed during the last forty years, which, in fact, when they get there, was just how it was changed. And she finds her two children there. Then she's taken back home, crying, "You can't take me away from my children!"

Shirdi Sai Baba

This was this amazing being, Shirdi Sai Baba, who had these incredible powers. He used to go down to the stream and pull out his intestines and wash them and hang them up in trees to dry. When an old couple came to him and cried because their money had been stolen and they couldn't get to see the Ganges River before they died, he said, "Don't worry about it." And the Ganges started to pour out of his toes.

He was known for having these incredible powers. He came to a little village, and at first they all ignored him. They wouldn't have anything to do with him because he was kind of weird. They wouldn't give him any oil for his lamp, so he just poured water into the lamp and it burned. That freaked them all out, so they started to worship him. It's the same thing of, "I give them what they want and I shake them up a bit, so then they'll want what I give." If you get people shaken a bit, they're open to the possibilities.

Those possibilities get pretty far out. Listen to this story about him: A woman's young son was bitten by a cobra and she cried out and begged Shirdi Sai Baba for sacred ash, but he did not give it and the child died. One of the oldest of the devotees implored him, "Baba! Her crying is heart-rending. For my sake, revive her son!"

Baba replied, "Do not get entangled in this. What has happened is for the best. He has already entered another body in which he can do especially good work, which he could not do in this one. If I draw him back into this body, then the new one he has entered will have to die for this one to live. I might do it for your sake, but have you considered the consequences? Have you any idea of the responsibility, and are you prepared to assume it?"

The Dialogue Between Heart and Mind

I once met a lama in New Jersey, a beautiful old man. He was so sweet to me, and he was so pure, and his heart was so lovely, and they were so poor.

I was driving from Newton to Millbrook. In the '60s we were moving our scene and I had a trailer full of stuff and a big Land Rover. We were connected with the Mellon family and we were rich, and these people were so poor, and my heart was touched by this man. I opened up the trunk of the trailer and I said, "Can you use this? How about these boards? Can you use this lamp? Can you use this rug?" I gave away just about everything in the trailer.

Even when I gave it all away, I still felt I hadn't given enough. I took out my checkbook and wrote out a check for everything that was in my account and I gave it to him. I drove away, and my mind said, "Are you out of your mind?" Which is exactly what I was – I was out of my mind. I'd gone into my heart and out of my mind.

That dialogue between the heart and the mind is an interesting one. The mind keeps saying, "Now don't give away the store. I mean, I hear about all the lilies in the field, but you're a human, and you've got taxes, and you've got mortgages, and you're going to get old and nobody's going to take care of you. Be careful."

And the heart keeps saying, "But . . . but . . .. ahhhh . . ." Because the heart is an instrument of unity, and the mind is an instrument of diversity.

The River of Thoughts

If you do meditation, you'll begin to notice your thoughts coming and going, if you don't grab at them. Each thought is saying, "Think of me. I'm important! Think of me. Think of me."

I've done meditation courses – so many meditation courses – where for ten days, from four in the morning until ten at night, you sit following your breath. Imagine that. You've gone to a foreign country, you sit down and you're waiting for these profound teachings. You're with 100 other people, and the teacher comes in and you all bow and wait for the instruction.

The teacher says, "You will feel the breath at the tip of the nose."

You go, sni-i-i-if, "Yeah, I got that."

"You will notice the breath going in when you breathe in, going by the nose. You will notice the breath going out when you breathe out."

"Got that. Yeah."

"It is like a doorkeeper. You watch the breath go in, you watch the breath go out."

"Yeah, okay. I got that."

And that's it! For ten days! And every little while he'll say, "Bring the attention back to the breath at the tip of the nose."

So you start, breathing in . . . breathing out . . . breathing in . . . This is never gonna work! Now the thought, This is never gonna work, is a thought, see? And it just said, "This is real! Think of me!"

You think, This is never gonna work, what am I doing here? How did I get into this? How am I gonna get out of it? Already you're off somewhere else.

And you'll hear, "Bring the awareness back to the breath."

But you think, Doesn't he realize how much my knee hurts! And then, I'm hungry. I wonder what we're going to have for lunch?

I found that at times I could have five- to six-hour fantasies. After a number of days – if you're lucky – you get tired of thinking and you start to rest in following the breath. Which is just a thought, by the way. But you're focusing on one thought to extricate yourself from this river of other thoughts that are going by you all the time, until you can let them go by like leaves floating down a stream, without having to get caught in each one, without identifying with being the thinker. The minute your mind starts to rest with one thought, it's like a laser beam. It burns through and cuts you into another space, which is like the space around the thought – like the blue skies behind the clouds, if clouds are thoughts that are crossing in the sky. In a moment, you are experiencing spaciousness, peace, presence, quietness, clarity.

Who's experiencing?

See, the minute you label who it is that's experiencing it, you're back in your thoughts again. "Who am I?" Any answer to that is just another thought. Because who you are isn't a conceptual thing – you aren't a thought. You're much richer. You are reducing yourself to your own thoughts. If you can't think about it, you decide you don't exist. Somehow you feel much more secure when you're in your thinking mind, because then you know you know. And there's something secure about knowing you know. But here we're dealing with a universe, and the nature of our being. You can be it, but you can't know it.

Climbing Mountains

I think most of us give lip service to the highest motives and the highest goals, but in truth that isn't what the thrust of our motivational efforts is. I think mainly we are aiming for a cessation of certain kinds of immediate suffering, and it's only when that cessation comes that you are ready.

It's like climbing mountains. You see the nearest mountain, you get to the top of it, then you see the next mountain. I don't think, though you give lip service to the highest kinds of aspirations – that I want to be free, I want liberation. Really, most people don't even know what the hell that's all about.

I was in the Vipassana Center and I'd meditated and meditated. Around the twelfth day of a 14-day course, I suddenly experienced a peace like I had never, ever experienced. I went rushing to Joseph, my meditation teacher, and said, "Joseph, I've got what I wanted. I've got peace." And he said, "Just follow your breath."

It took me a while to realize what he was saying because I'd always yearned for peace. And then I saw that peace was just another place, and I had to just keep going.

Sasaki Roshi

My introduction to the Zen koan was at a Benedictine Monastery in Elmira, New York. There was a gathering of holy beings, and we all were taking turns doing our trips. It was about four in the morning and I was sitting next to Swami Satchitananda and Swami Venketeshananda. We were all being taken through a Zen sitting by Sasaki Roshi, who is a very fierce Japanese teacher of a form of Zen that uses the koan – the insoluble riddle.

After he had taught us how to sit (which is in an incredibly tense position), he said, "Now, how you know your Buddha nature through sound of cricket?" What you're supposed to do is think about that as you're sitting in this miserably uncomfortable position at four in the morning. You're supposed to keep saying to yourself, "How do I know my Buddha nature through the sound of a cricket?" And you think, and you think, and you think.

Then you get called in for dokasan – a personal meeting with the teacher. There's a form to it: You come in, you bow and you scrape, and you touch the floor so many times, and then you sit down on the student cushion. He's sitting with a bell and a stick. "Ahhh, doctor. Doctor, how you know your Buddha nature through sound of cricket?"

Well, I'd been working for hours getting ready for this moment, and I had arrived at a plan. What I decided I'd do was, when he asked the question, I would hold up my hand like Milarepa does, sitting in front of the cave listening to the universe. I figured I'll throw him a Tibetan answer, since I'm a Jewish Hindu and he's Japanese, and it'll it least confuse him if nothing else. I'll at least show him a little bit.

So I held up my hand. and he picked up his bell, rang it, and said, "60 percent." Which completely sucked me in, of course; a Jewish achiever has got to get the other 40 percent!

Sometime later on, I found myself in a sauna bath in Santa Fe, New Mexico, with a Tibetan nun, Allen Ginsberg, and Bhagawan Das. It was a colorful group of people sitting around naked in this sauna bath, and I'm in total Sensual-ville. I had come planning to spend about two weeks just lying around. A telegram arrived for me that said, "There will be a Rohatsu Diasesshin," and it gave the starting date, which was two days later. The telegram said, "This is the most difficult sesshin of the year. It will go on for nine days. we have reserved a place for you."

Now this is Sasaki Roshi's scene, right? And I thought, "Oh, God! Nine days of that?" But there was something in it . . .

I called them immediately and said, "Well, I'm only a beginner and that's for advanced students. Thank you so much for thinking of me, and I certainly would like to sit with you some time."

They said, "Oh, you can do it." Which got me in the next vulnerable place, so I found myself a few hours later on a plane to Los Angeles. After a long trip I arrived at the Zen Center up on Mt. Baldy. I was met by a fellow with a shaved head in a black robe who handed me a towel, a black robe, and a pillow, and said, "Dass, Ram. You will be in the upper bunk in cabin four. You will be in the zendo in five minutes, in your robe."

Nobody says, "Gee, Ram Dass, great that you came." Not one tiny bit of ego feeding in the whole thing.

I walk into the zendo, and there's a cushion with "Dass" on the back of it. I sit down and they teach us how to sit. What then begins is something that is hard to believe goes on in America 30 miles from Los Angeles. We start every morning at 2 a.m. and go until 10 p.m., so we had four hours of sleep. It was really very cold at the top of the mountain, there was even snow on the ground at times.

We got up at two, and had five minutes to wake up, wash, and be in the zendo. Once you sat down in the zendo and the bell rang, you could not move. There was a man walking back and forth – a tough-looking guy with a big stick – and if you moved he came up to you and hit the floor with the stick. Now everybody knew you'd been caught, see? Then he turned and bowed to you, and you would bow to him, and then you'd lean down and he'd beat you three times on one shoulder; then you'd lean the other way and he'd beat you three times on that shoulder. And he beat you – it really stung for about fifteen minutes afterwards! Then you thanked him, and he thanked you, and you went back into your position.

It didn't have to be a gross thing that you did. I mean, imagine that you just woke up and your sinuses are full. You're sitting there, and the mucus starts to drip out of your nose and down over your moustache and down your beard. You go, "Sniff!" That would do it. The first day you might get a "shhh." But the second day, you'd get the stick. If you need to go to the bathroom, you get up and go to the guy and whisper, "I need to go to the bathroom." And he says, "Be quick!" You run out, and you can't go because you're so nervous that you won't get back in time!

You're given a koan by Sasaki Roshi, and you see him five times a day. Five times a day he asks you your koan, and you give him your answer that you've thought up. And he gives you responses like this: First time he just says, "No," and rings the bell. Later he gets into subtleties like, "Oh, doctor. I expected more of you than that." That's a nice one!

You walk out and you think, "Well, screw him. I'm gonna leave. I don't need to stay here!" By the third day I was really sick. My back had gone out of joint, and I was thinking that what I really needed was an osteopath and maybe I ought to leave because, after all, if your back is out . . . And I was totally, wildly paranoid. I felt they were out to get me. Because the guy next to me they didn't beat at all. Me, a professional holy man, they were whipping left and right!

About the fifth day I was totally paranoid and up tight. Nobody had given me one bit of warmth. Finally I was so uptight and so furious that I realized I didn't give a damn about the koan. I walked in to Sasaki Roshi and he said, "How you know . . ." Whatever it was he was asking me those days.

I couldn't care less how I'd know, and I said, "Good morning, Roshi."

"Ah," he said, "Now you are becoming a beginning student of Zen."

I went out and I was walking two feet off the ground – I'd just solved the koan! Which made the next two days even more horrible than the first four had been. But finally by the seventh day I was so stoned by the whole scene that the bushes all had flames coming out of them. The whole place had a luminous quality, and no matter which koan he gave me the answers were coming out right. We were going through koan after koan, and it was all just exquisite.

Uncle Richard Is Evil

I've got to tell you an interesting story. There was a time in 1964 or 1965 when Tim Leary and I had been partners for several years. We got to the point where we were disagreeing about strategies, and we separated for a while. But we still had a joint involvement, because I was the treasurer and director of the corporation, and we were running Millbrook in New York.

I got back from Europe and came to Millbrook. Timothy was then running Millbrook – I had been running it for the year previously when he had been away in India – and Timothy and I were at great odds (which we've since reconciled to a much deeper love). I was at that point the legal guardian of his children, because he had been away and I was very close to his kids. He came to his kids one night while I was sitting there and said, "Kids, I have to tell you this: Uncle Richard," which is who I was then, "Uncle Richard is evil."

Now Timothy had a good Catholic upbringing, and that might have meant something to him; it didn't mean a helluva lot to me. His son said to him, "Oh, come on Dad! He may be a shnook, but he's not evil."

Timothy said, "No, no. Uncle Richard is evil."

Of course, I lost my cool at that point (which I was very good at doing in those days) and I said to him, "Well, Timothy, if I'm evil, you're psychotic." Which got to him, as I knew it would, and we were both totally freaked.

Well, I left Millbrook at that time and went to California. But what he said started to work on my head. "You know, I've done an awful lot of rotten things in my life. Do you suppose I am evil? Do you suppose there's something basically corrupt and rotten in me?"

In the fall I was with a gal – we'd been together for a while, and we took LSD together one night. Right in the middle of the session I said, "You know, Timothy thinks I'm evil." So in the state we were in at that moment, she looked at me and what I turned into I can't imagine, but she said, "Well, maybe you are!" Well, that was the end of that relationship. I became impotent, and she ran off with another man.

So I kept working with this problem: Do you suppose I'm evil? Gee, I must be. I guess maybe I'm really evil. Then around February of that year I took a very deep acid trip by myself, and I went in and in. I went to where I really felt evil; I stood in front of a mirror and became as evil as I could, and I went through all my evil thoughts. I really scared the hell out of myself (literally!).

I went back and back and back, and I came to a place in me where I just am. I do a lot of crummy things, and I do a lot of beautiful things, and I'm neither good nor evil. I just am. There's good, there's evil, and I am. I realize that's true of everybody, but suddenly that was a recognition again of it for me. I'd touched it before, but I had never had the predicament where my best friend said, "You're evil," so I'd never had the opportunity to work as intensely with it as this.

So from then on, I was really quite liberated from that whole issue of good and evil, which I have been ever since (except in subtle ways, where it sneaks back in on me).

It was about a year and a half later. Tim had been busted in Laredo and we had set up the defense fund. We were still very cold, but we were working together. I was then living in New York City, and one night we got a call. It was about two in the morning. It was the people at Millbrook, and they said, "Tim's taken a chemical, and he's been calling for you all night." I hadn't seen him in six months or so.

So the next morning we rented a car and drove up to Millbrook, and I came to see Timothy. I walked into the room, and Timothy was lying on the floor. He got up and came over and embraced me, and he said, "I just want you to know one thing."

I said, "What's that, Timothy?"

He said, "You're not evil."

I said, "Well, thank you. I already found that out. But I appreciate what you did for me. Because if you hadn't laid that trip on me, I never would have done that work."

Even though it was incredibly painful, that suffering was incredible grace in terms of my own evolution. And the quicker you can get the perception where you understand that suffering is grace, the more you're going to have all of it become the teaching.

The Hippie Postman

I knew this very beautiful guy who took a lot of acid, got all uptight and all strung out on am-
phetamines, and went through the whole trip. He was in Haight-Ashbury and was all weird,
and I was dealing with him in the middle of the night, with all kinds of hysteria and mental
hospitals and dramas. Then a few years later I got a note from him, that he's living with his
chick in a little country town, and he's the postman. He wrote, "It's such a groove to go on
my route every day."

You mean you went through college to become a postman?

Before satori you chop wood and carry water. After satori you chop wood and carry water.
That's what is emerging, very slowly. It's not that the outside drama changes. It's not that fam-
ilies aren't created. It's not that business doesn't go on. It's not that legal problems don't exist.
It's not that society doesn't have its games and rules and laws. It's a question of how conscious
the beings are who are doing it. Because if a person has surrendered their ego, then they do what
is in harmony with the universe.

And what is the universe? It's your biochemistry, it's your skills, it's your heredity, it's your
environment, it's all of the forces acting upon you at that moment. It's all the moral possibilities
around you. That's all part of what the harmony of the universe is.

Our Collective Mind

One day I was sitting on the front lawn of my father's farm in New Hampshire. He has a very big, fancy place. I was alone there, living in a little cabin behind the house. I was sitting naked in the front yard at sunset, doing asanas. A little Volkswagen drove up, and I saw two people get out of the car. A box of stuff was thrown out, and the Volkswagen drove away. I'm way out in the country, and usually nobody visits me after a certain time, but there they were.

They walked over to me and sat down. I said, "Hello. Would you like some tea?"

The man – he was in his early twenties – said, "Yes. We'll take some."

So I got up, put on my pants, and I went in and made some tea. I brought out the tea and some cups and a bowl of figs. I set it down; I thought we'd have tea at sunset. He took the bowl of figs and threw the figs on the ground so her could fill the bowl with tea – he wanted to drink his tea out of the bowl. Then he put a fig in his mouth and chewed it up, then spit it into his girl's mouth. Not a word had been said during all this. I was just drinking my tea . . .

I realized that it was sunset and obviously they weren't going anywhere, the car had driven away. I had this big house, so I said, "I live in the cabin in back of the house, but my father has said I can use the back room and the back bathroom. I don't use the rest of the house, because that's his trip. If you'd like to stay in that room, okay."

The fellow said, "Well, we'll look at it." So I carried his box upstairs, settled him down. They said they were satisfied and would take the room for the night.

I said, "I'm going to cook dinner up at the cabin. I'll ring a bell. You can come up for dinner if you want, it's just rice and stuff, but if you want you can come up."

I cooked dinner, rang the bell, and she came up. I said, "Isn't your friend coming?"

She said, "No, he's afraid to leave the suitcase. He's afraid someone will steal it."

Okay . . . So we ate dinner, and I sent some food with her for him.

Around 10:30 p.m. I went down to see that everything was all right. It all seemed cool. I offered them a joint; we smoked a joint together, very loving. I said, "Well, I'm going to bed. Here's your room. Your bathroom is downstairs. These doors we keep closed – that's my father's part of the house. Good night." I went to the cabin and went to sleep.

Around 3 a.m. I heard this screaming: "I will not stand for this!" I sat up and looked out of my cabin window, and in the house, every light in the whole house was on. So I got up and went down to the house.

He had gone through the house and systematically taken all the drawers and turned them upside

106

down; he had taken chalk and written all over the walls; he had put ink into the sinks; he had put ketchup into the piano. He had on three pairs of my father's pants and three shirts. So I surveyed the whole scene.

Now, you've got a choice in this situation. You could call the police, but that's kind of heavy, and after all it's all done now. The best thing to do is just sit there. If I sit there the rest of the night, what more can he do if I'm right there? I mean, I'm a student of karate! So I sit down in the middle of the living room and start to meditate, figuring, "I'll just fill the place with such good vibrations that it'll cool him out."

He comes down and sees me looking really holy. He's got his diary, and he sits down and says, "Well, this is a very comfortable place. I think I'll stay four or five days." And it blew my cool completely! My whole holy cover was very thin anyway.

I said, "Like hell you will, you son of a bitch! You'll be out of here tomorrow morning!" He just looked at me and laughed, and laughed, and laughed. He went upstairs and went into the bathroom and locked the door.

I was so freaked; my bones and my muscles and my back were all tight. I had to do asanas, and breathing, and deeper breathing. It took me about half an hour to get my center back. Then I went up and knocked on the door.

He opened it and said, "What do you want?"

I said, "I want to thank you. You're a very great teacher."

He said, "Too many people have been calling me the Buddha!" There's not an inch in the whole story! So he said, "Get in that room!" I go in the room. He said, "Sit down on the bed!" I sat down on the bed. "Sit in the lotus! Don't be a slob!!" I got in lotus position. Then he sat down opposite me.

That was around 4:30 a.m. The next thing I remember it was about seven. The meditation was one of the deepest meditations that I ever remember having.

I came out of the meditation and said to him, "Would you like a cup of tea?" He said yes, so I went downstairs. By the time I got back he was totally wild again. He demanded a new suitcase and all. I said, "Well, here's your tea. It's time to leave now."

He said, "Well, I'm not going!"

I said, "Oh yes you are."

"No I'm not!"

I took his arm and put it around his back and gently urged him into the car, took him to the State Highway and said, "Well, here's where you start to thumb."

I let them out and the girl said, "I don't want to go with him." Okay. You can take a bus from town. She said, "But he's wearing my fur coat."

I said, "May I have the coat?" So he swung at me. I took his arm and put it around his back; slowly we took off the coat, and we left him with his box of laundry by the side of the highway and drove away.

I loved him so much! He got about 30 miles away, and apparently whoever picked him up got frightened, and he ended up in the Concord Hospital. He called me from the hospital, and from then on he called me roughly every night for the next two weeks. He jumped out of the fourth floor window of the Concord Hospital and escaped, and he just went from place to place. But the love between us was incredibly strong.

Since then I've heard from him about once a year. He's now married, and has a whole different scene going – he's very settled. But I use that as another example of the phenomenon of dealing with our collective mind, and working with the stuff that comes along, no matter how weird or jarring it may be.

Nityananda and Desire

Nityananda was big and fat like Maharajji, and he'd sit on a stone wall. He'd hardly ever speak; he grunted. He was an extraordinary being; the shakti was intense. He did seven years of "monkey tapasya," standing in a tree. You really have to have the calling for that. But he got so he dropped leaves on people, and the leaves would heal them. I guess you do develop something if you stand in a tree.

Later on, he'd sit there on a wall and people would line up to see him. This story's always perplexed me, because they'd come up and say, "Nityanada, is American Telephone a good investment for this week?"

He'd go, "Hhrrmph!" And they'd go out and invest and make a lot of money.

I thought, What a funny use for spiritual powers!

But when you go back and back and back, what are you so upset about? You don't care. Let each person get what they want – until they want something other than what they thought they wanted. Because if you push away what you want prematurely, like, "I'm gonna get disciplined" – that one – if you do it prematurely, you'll still have a lurking desire for a little bit more of whatever it was.

I always push people back under. They come and they say, "I'm really trying to give up smoking dope, so I can go to God."

I say, "No. Smoke some more."

VP of Industrial Loans

I was at a meditation retreat. We hadn't started yet, so we could talk for those few minutes before the retreat began. I said to the fellow who was in one of the other bunks in the room, "What do you do?"

He said, "I'm a vice president in a bank in San Francisco, in charge of industrial loans. But it's an interesting story. I was a vice president in a San Francisco bank in charge of industrial loans ten years ago. Then I couldn't handle it anymore, so I dropped out, left my family and left the job. I went off and took a lot of acid, and I wrote poetry and lived in communes. I did that for about eight years."

"Then one day," he said, "I was walking through San Francisco, and I met the president of the bank. He said, 'Gee, isn't it amazing that I met you today? It turns out that your desk is open again, and you were the best vice president of industrial loans we ever had. Would you consider coming back?' And I thought, Why not? So I shaved off my beard, got my tie and the whole thing, and I went to work."

I said, "Well, is it any different?"

He said, "It's entirely different! Before, I used to be a vice president in charge of industrial loans. Now I'm a being that goes to this place and hangs out with people all day long. We're together. And the vehicle for us to be together is industrial loans."

So instead of hating the job because of his identification, he's now seeing it as a vehicle, if you can think of a less appealing vehicle from the spiritual point of view. I would find it hard because people come wanting something from you very materially. Yet in every situation is the opportunity to meet a living spirit . . . if you are looking with eyes that see.

Cruise on the Luraleen

I used to go traveling with my father and stepmother. They were really pretty groovy, but I'd watch how they could take something that is absolutely quite beautiful and make it into a living hell.

Years ago I went by ship – the Luraleen – from San Francisco to Hawaii. I had a deck chair that had on one side of it the smokestack from the kitchen, with the smell of grease coming by my nose, and on the other side sat my father, with a cigar. It was almost impossible to get a smell of the ocean if I sat in my deck chair, because it was constantly either grease or cigar smoke going by my face.

I remember how I was busy having it destroy my whole trip. I ruined the whole trip with complaints about this and that: about who was at our table . . . about the fact that my tuxedo had a stain nobody could see, but I knew about it . . . about how sexually frustrated I was . . . about how would I escape from my parents . . . all of these things that my mind was full of!

When people say, "Have you changed at all?" I think, Boy, have I changed! I can take any situation now, open to it and say, "Yeah. Okay." Now that doesn't mean I won't enjoy softness, and I won't enjoy love, and I won't enjoy luxury, but enjoying it and needing it for one's happiness are two entirely different things. There is a tremendous shift in perception of what life is about when you can create as beautiful a life as you can, and then take what comes down the road and work with it joyfully, even when it's heavy and negative stuff.

A Scientist and a Datum

I decided at one stage of the game to open Pandora's Box and let it all in, and whatever would float would float. I even remember when it happened. It was back at Harvard, and Tim Leary and I were doing research on psychedelics under the umbrella of Harvard.

Harvard was getting a little concerned because we had just ordered a half million dollars worth of LSD from Switzerland, and they set up a watchdog committee, which was unheard of, for faculty members to watch over each other. I was on that committee, with other men, and we couldn't agree on anything.

Finally some of the faculty had a public meeting in order to put down our work. The thrust of the meeting was that we were not scientific – mainly because we were ingesting these chemicals ourselves. How could you be a scientist when you were changing your perceptual viewpoint in the midst of your observational study?

Now there is a very rich tradition in psychology called "Introspectionism," but it's in very low repute because of the takeover by Behaviorism. Behaviorism bought physics as a model for human study, and therefore rejected all inner experience other than what could be said outwardly and written down and then studied – as written material, not as what happened inside.

Then Timothy took the stand and said, "I am a scientist. You people don't understand what science is." Timothy happens to be a damned good philosopher of science, and I think he had a very good argument. He protested that they were persecuting science because of their own position.

I was experiencing being caught in the middle of the situation. The most powerful things that had ever happened to me were happening every Saturday night, and somehow that was more real to me than what I was doing teaching Freudian psychodynamics on Monday, Wednesday, and Friday. I was not sure that I could bring that stuff together at that point, and I took a stance quite different from Timothy.

I said, "You're absolutely right, gentlemen. I am no longer a scientist. I'm turning in my badge. From now on I should be considered a datum. And you may study me to see what happened to me in the '60s. 'Too bad about poor Dick' – that one. You can study and you can be the scientists. You can have the role. I give it up, because I don't really want it anymore."

Because it's a drag! If I take that role, everything that comes near me I've got to say, "Well, will I accept it? What is the probability of its reoccurrence? How many sigma deviations . . ." See? I've got to live in a probabilistic model, and sit with the skeptical stance of doubt, which always keeps me a certain distance from the "here." Because I've always got to be one thought away.

I realized I didn't want to be one thought away from life anymore. I wanted to dive into the soup and the hell with it – whatever would happen would happen. I wanted to get to the point where when I sit in a village in India and people tell me stories about miracles that would turn the hair of Westerners gray, I can say, "Yeah! Of course! Far out!" And I can mean it. As far as I'm concerned, it's all true. If it isn't, that's its problem and not mine.

Now before that at Harvard, I was a member of a group of Young Turks in the Social Relations Department who were trying to toughen up the department with more statistics requirements and experimental methodology. At that time, when parapsychological phenomena occurred, I would say, "Very interesting. We certainly must keep an open mind." That was my professional position.

Then I started to take psychedelics and all these things started to happen to me. I said, "I have ingested a psychotropic agent and I am having a hallucination and it's fascinating." Then, a lot like what Carl Jung does in Memories, Dreams and Reflections, I said, "Fortunately I can come back to my family and my home and to reality." That was another stage.

As time went on it became less and less clear which one I was coming back to. Then as I stopped worrying about that – which made you very edgy in terms of mental health – phenomena started to occur to me when I was not under a psychedelic, and I had no recourse to the fact that it hadn't happened to me but to somebody else, so I couldn't use the scientific one of "very interesting, we must keep an open mind," because it had just happened to me.

So I was left without a defense. There is a predicament about the phrase, "Blessed are your eyes for they see and your ears for they hear" – that there are phenomena which are available to her who has not veiled herself from them through attachment to her own thought.

All of it is available to everybody, but it depends on who you think you are as to whether or not it is available to you.

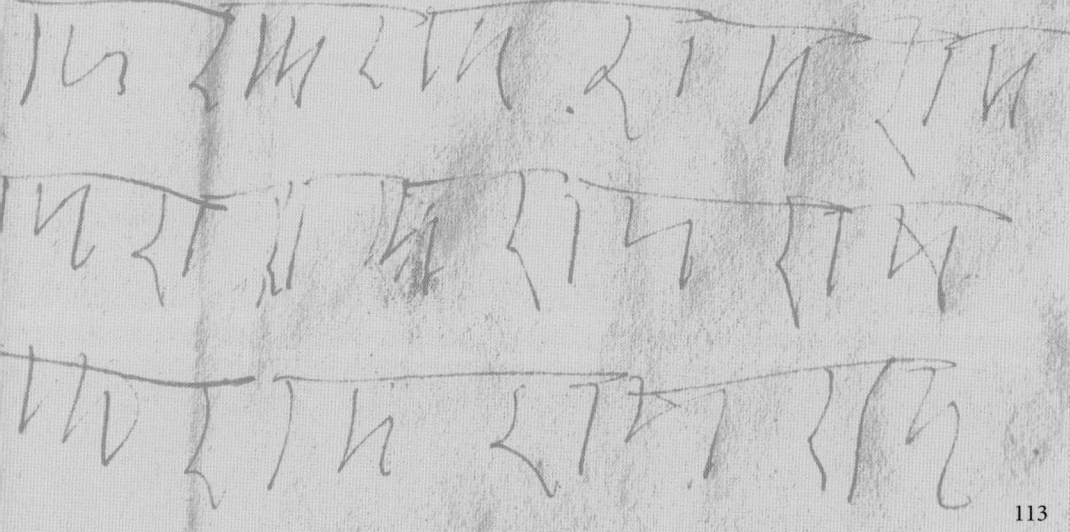

113

Mid-America Motel Trip

I have had certain acid trips that have demanded that I surrender. I had an LSD trip at the Mid-America Motel in Salinas, Kansas. I had just left Trungpa Rinpoche, and I was carrying some thangkas out to Boulder. I had visited this underground acid producer, and he had given me this stuff that shone in the dark! I had five days before I had to appear in Boulder. My guru had said I could take the yogi medicine if I was in a cool place, I was feeling peace, my heart was turned towards God, and I was alone – all those conditions happened to be fulfilled at the Mid-America Motel.

So I put the thangkas around the motel room, and put questions around the room that I'd like to ask myself when I met me later. I had a picture of Maharajji in the middle of the television screen and turned it on without the sound, so all these images were coming out of his head. I made the room beautiful with incense and candles, and got it nice and warm. I took all off my clothes and took the acid.

Well, it turned out the acid was much stronger than what I thought I was taking. I thought it was 200 micrograms and probably it was something like 2,000 micrograms – I don't know. In my scientific rigor, it was what would stick to the end of a matchstick. You know how reliable that is. Whatever it was, long after I should have peaked I was still on my way out, and I realized that whatever happened was too much.

I went in to pee, and by the time I had finished peeing I had peed the universe, and I had scared the living hell out of myself! I decided I was about to die. That's known as Grade B paranoia; it's called a bad trip. I rushed to the door to get help. I had my hand on the door, and the whole image came to me of what scenario was about to ensue: this naked bald man in Room 125 running up to the manager saying, "I'm going to die!" And then I thought of the police, and the psychiatrists and the Thorazine, and I decided there had to be a better way to die than this.

I closed the door and came back into the room.

I was desperately trying to find a way not to die, but the problem was that everything I thought of ended in death. I mean, it might take 40 years, but sooner or later it was going to end in death, no matter which choice I made. It was absolutely inevitable.

I was rushing around the room, panicked because I was going to die, when I caught sight of Maharajji's image. So I said to Maharajji, "Okay. There's no way out. I don't want to prolong it. Let me die. I'm ready, let's do it now." I lay down on the floor to die. I imagined them finding my body the next day, you know? With all these signs around, like:

"What is God?"

"What is Truth?"

"Love is . . ."

And this naked old man lying in front of television set with a picture glued on it.

I thought, "Well, I'm really leaving a legacy for the community: 'Ram Dass Found Naked and Drugged in Mid-America Motel.'"

Then my awareness started to pull back from my mind, and I saw my thoughts getting slower, and slower, and slower, until I saw each thought arising, existing, and passing away. As it disappeared, the whole universe would disappear. Then it came to the point where there was this space between the thoughts. I came up to one of them, and I let my awareness go into the space between the thoughts. I felt this "snap" in my consciousness. It was like a discontinuous moment and, at that moment, I wasn't.

The next thought I had was, "Well, now you can be anything you want this time around." At that moment I had seen that the only thing that was going to die was the thought of who I was. I had been nothing, and here I am – and all the time I had been frightened of being nothing. I realized that that had been given to me, and I went into states of bliss. That feeling has hung in with me and it's made a difference, because I now understand that what that is is nothing my mind can conceive of, and yet it is.

Well, after I pulled back from the void, Maharajji appeared and manifested in the exact way that's written about in the eleventh chapter of the Bhagavad Gita, where the entire universe is the skin of his body. The room was filled with the entire universe, and Maharajji kept turning into all these other beings and absorbing them all, just changing and changing. He was sitting on the bed laughing, and all this stuff was going in and out of him.

So I can see that partly through the drugs, partly through meditation, partly through being around Maharajji, partly through steeping myself in the Gospel of Sri Ramakrishna and teachings of the Visuddhimagga, and on and on and on, that there has developed in me some kind of calmness and presence, allowing me to know that death is not an enemy – it's merely another point in the transition.

Arrows and Hearts

At one point I was with Tim Leary and we were doing Saturday Night Research, as usual. It was New Year's Eve, and a group of us took LSD. New Year's Day was my parents' 40th Anniversary. My mother was already sick with cancer, and my brothers and I had spent many months preparing a beautiful album of their married life together, with pictures and poetry and art. I had it, and was to present it.

I had timed the taking of the acid a little wrong. I'd been up all night, and in the morning when I went to shave, there was no face in the mirror. I thought, Well, don't scare yourself. It's okay. Just close your eyes and shave. I did that, because I couldn't let down my parents – that would be out of the question. I got in the car to drive and the steering wheel kept turning into a snake and the people on the street spoke a foreign language. I was scaring the hell out of myself, but I thought, Don't get scared. You're just going to your brother's.

I got there and went into the house. I was wearing sunglasses, which they understood, because on New Year's Eve you're allowed in the culture to get drunk, so I was "hung over" and I could play "being hung over" – a role to handle my slightly disoriented way. Because when I walked into the door, what I saw was that all of my family were monkeys. They were all on different branches around the house. My grandmother was this little old monkey with sagging breasts, and my little niece monkeys were running around, and everybody was scratching and watching me. I was saying, "Hi! Hello! Great to see you. Let me hug you." I was hugging these monkeys, it was very weird.

We sat down to brunch. My brother was sitting across from me, and in a particular kind of Jewish family like ours, love is often expressed through a kind of ribbing that's right on the edge of something that really cuts. So my brother looked over at me and said, "Well, how's the nut business?" (I was a psychologist in those days.)

And I saw . . . out of his mouth came an arrow, and it very slowly came across the table to-wards me. With my mind, I very gently reached up and took the arrow and put it down next to my spoon. Then I took a heart and I blew it to him. I said, "You know Bill, you and your wife are looking better all the time. You must have a great marriage." The heart went across, and a look of confusion spread across his face because that isn't the rule of the game!

He tried again and said, "Well, whatever you're learning, it's not growing any hair!" Another arrow came across, and I put it down next to the first one.

I sent him another heart, saying, "Gee, Bill, your children are getting so incredible. I really am impressed with how it's been going." And again the look of confusion.

All I remember about that day is that in the afternoon we all were sitting around the liv-ing room, everybody on everybody's lap, everybody feeling this weird sort of thing that we weren't saying but were all experiencing: Is this really our family? What had happened was the entire family had gotten a contact high, and we were all out there together. We got out to the street at the end of the day and nobody wanted to get into their car to drive away. You know what that feels like, how it goes on for hours because nobody can bear to be parted? I kept thinking, This isn't my family. I always could bear to be parted from them!

The next day I thought, Well, maybe I just thought it was beautiful, because of where my consciousness was. But they were all saying, "What a family! What a beautiful family we have!" I saw about forgiveness, and about anger. When people send stuff in your direction, if you'll quiet down you don't have to be reactive. You don't have to keep the karmic chains going. You can just receive it, allow it, appreciate it, and then be with the new moment in an honest way. It keeps shifting gears, and it's quite extraordinary to watch.

The Maharajji Blanket

I was with Swami Muktananda in Melbourne, Australia, and everybody was bringing so many gifts to him. Now my guru, like Nityananda, was really hard to bring anything to, because they weren't that kind of manifestation. You'd bring Maharajji some apples, and he'd take them and throw them at people. But some of the old Indian devotees would come and bring blankets for him, see, because he had a blanket. And then sometimes, if they were really lucky, he'd take their blanket and he'd give them the blanket he was wearing. Then they'd have one of Maharajji's blankets to have at home.

I was the elder of the Western devotees, and I was in Australia with Muktananda on the way to Maharajji in India, and I thought, I wonder if I could give him a blanket. Usually the Westerners just give him apples, because we never thought we were "inside" enough to be able to give him a blanket. But I thought, Well, I'll give him a blanket.

I went to a big department store and I got a beautiful mohair blanket – it was even in a plastic case. I came back and Swami Muktananda was standing on the steps and said, "Ah, what is that?"

I said, "It's a blanket for my guru."

He said, "Oh, very good."

Everybody said, "That's Ram Dass's blanket for his guru," and we all carried it, it was on airplanes, and it became "THE blanket."

I got up to Nainital, and Maharajji wasn't there. So I got my friends, who ran a hotel, to put it in their safe because this was THE blanket, and I had visions that I was going to get the blanket he was wearing.

Five months later, Maharajji, the blanket, and I were finally all in the same town at the same moment. The time had come! I get the blanket out of the hotel safe, take the bus to the temple, come in to the room where we're all sitting in front of Maharajji. There's Krishna Das and Rameshwar Das and Dwarka and Jeff and Jim, and there's Danny Goleman, who's just come from a meditation course, with a new girlfriend he met at the course. This is her first time visiting Maharajji. And everybody knows that this is the moment for the presentation of the blanket.

Maharajji is talking to everybody; we're all sitting there. I come in with the blanket and kneel down and I put the blanket down next to him on the takhat. He's talking to somebody. Finally his eyes focus on the blanket, and he looks at it for a moment. Then he reaches out and he picks it up like he was picking up a dead rat, and he throws it at the girl. Says, "That's for you."

Then he turns to me and says, "Was that the right thing to do?"

I said to him, "Perfect."

That couple got married and had two kids. The kids were raised in the blanket – "The Maharajji Blanket." Then the couple split up and the blanket got lost in transit. Nobody could find it. They each remarried and moved very close together and they've all become very loving and good friends. It's an incredibly beautiful extended family now, and the kids are blossoming. When it all got cooled out, a box was found that had the blanket in it.

So I'm just watching that blanket. It's like the last convertible. You watch the story of how it keeps moving through the universe.

Glossary

Asanas – Sanskrit, the physical postures in hatha yoga

Bij – Sanskrit, seed syllable, like "om" or "ram"

Chakra – Sanskrit, energy center

Chapatis – Hindi, thin, round, unleavened Indian bread

Chutzpah – Yiddish, audacity, guts

Darshan – Sanskrit, the sight or presence of a holy person

Dharma – Sanskrit, the righteousness of duty in accord with cosmic order

Dhoti – Hindi, a garment worn by men, a sinple piece of material tried around waist,
	coving most of the legs

Ektara – Hindi, one-stringed instrument made from a gourd

Ghat – Hindi, a flight of stairs leading down to a river

Hanuman – Sanskrit, a Hindu monkey-like deity, whose exploits are described in the Ramayana

Karma – Sanskrit, the sum of actions from previous lives and this life that determine the future

Koan – in Zen Buddhism, a paradoxical riddle for going beyond the logical mind

Kedgeree – Hindi, a simple Indian dish of rice and lentils

Krishna – Sanskrit, one of the main Hindu deities, an incarnation of love

Kundalini -- Sanskrit, the feminine energy coiled at the base of the spine

Mahasamadhi – Sanskrit, the final samadhi, consciously and intentionally leaving one's body

Mandala – Sanskrit, a geometric circular figure representing the universe

Mantra – Sanskrit, a word or sound repeated to aid concentration, especially in meditation

Mudra – Sanskrit, symbolic hand gestures

Namaste – Sanskrit, a common respectful greeting in India, loosely meaning "I honor the
	light within you."

Pranayama – Sanskrit, breathing techniques

Raja yoga – Sanskrit, the "kingly" yoga for achieving control over the mind and emotions

Sadhana – Sanskrit, literally "a means of accomplishing something," spiritual exercise aimed at the ultimate expression of one's life

Sadhu – Sanskrit, a holy man, sage, or ascetic

Samadhi – Sanskrit, final stage of concentration reaching union with the divine

Samskaras – Sanskrit the individual impressions, ideas, and actions that make up our conditioning

Satori – Japanese, sudden enlightenment

Sattvic – Sanskrit, pure

Sesshin – Japanese, literally "touching the heart-mind," a period of intensive meditation (zazen) in Zen monastery

Shaktipat – Sanskrit, the transfer of spiritual energy from teacher to student to awaken kundalini

Shanti -- Sanskrit, peace

Shiva – Hebrew, week-long period of mourning for first-degree relatives, "sitting shiva."

Shnook – Yiddish, a fool

Shul – Yiddish, temple

Sunyasin – Sanskrit, renunciate

Sushumna – Sanskrit, the channel of subtle life force energy

Takhat – Hindi, a wooden platform

Tapasya – Sanskrit, disciplined spiritual practice to reach self-realization

Thangkas – Tibetan Buddhist painting, usually depicting a Buddhist deity, scene, or mandala

Theravadan – a major tradition of Buddhism

Yoga – Sanskrit, union (through spiritual and ascetic discipline)

Zendo – Japanese meditation hall